Cushions
& Covers

READER'S DIGEST

PRACTICAL HOME DECORATING

Cushions & Covers

A Step-by-Step Guide to Creative Soft Furnishings

Gina Moore

Photographs by
Michael Crockett and Geoff Dann

READER'S DIGEST ASSOCIATION, INC.
Pleasantville, New York/Montreal

A READER'S DIGEST BOOK

Conceived, edited, and designed by
COLLINS & BROWN LIMITED

Library of Congress Cataloging in Publication Data

Moore, Gina.
    Cushions & covers: a step-by-step guide to creative pillow covers, tablecloths,
and seat coverings / Gina Moore.
        p.   cm. — (Practical home decorating)
    Includes index.
    ISBN 0-89577-980-3
    1. Cushions.   2. Pillows.   3. Household linens.   4. Textile fabrics in interior decoration.
fabrics in interior decoration.   I. Title.   II. Series.
    TT387.M66 1997
    746.9—dc21   97-22201

Editorial Director: Colin Ziegler
Art Director: Roger Bristow
Designer: Suzanne Metcalfe-Megginson
Photography by Geoff Dann and Michael Crockett
Styling by Maya Babic
Illustrations by Ian Sidaway

Printed in Italy

CONTENTS

The Basic Techniques

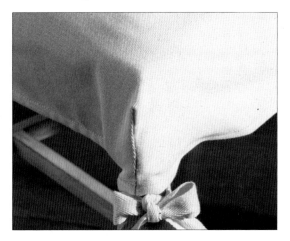

The Projects

INTRODUCTION

MAKING YOUR OWN cushions and covers provides a marvellous opportunity to explore the beauty and versatility of fabric. As accessories to a decorating scheme, cushions and covers add style, color, and texture as much as comfort and practicality. A few well-placed scatter cushions in jewel-bright silk enliven a bland, neutral living room; a pale damask cover on an upright chair lifts a dark, heavy dining room; and throws and cushions can soften a stark bedroom, adding warmth to a cool setting or cool accents to a warm one.

Because cushions can be moved around and covers changed as the mood and season dictates, you can be adventurous and experimental. What's more, since the quantities of fabric needed are relatively small, you can afford to be extravagant, using the more lavish fabrics and trimmings that are only usually considered for larger projects, such as curtains or upholstery. So, whether you are planning to redecorate from scratch or to revamp the decor in an existing room, let this book be an introduction to the world of textiles and the way they can transform an interior to create a particular style or mood.

When you have decided on your project by assessing the furniture you wish to work on (see pp. 8–11), turn to the pages on color, pattern, and texture (see pp. 14–19), then begin the search for suitable fabrics that catch your eye. Let your personal taste be the final arbiter on the fabrics you select, but be open to surprises. Collect as many varied samples as you can, then start the exciting process of combining fabrics to create contrasting and harmonious effects (see pp. 14–15). If you have never done this before, you will be sure to enjoy the process of working with fabric and to discover just how spontaneous and rewarding the results can be.

Simple sewing techniques are clearly illustrated and explained at the beginning of this book (see pp. 32–47) to provide instant reference as you work through the projects. The projects (see pp. 48–123) are designed to cover a wide range of furniture – from fitted squab and box cushions, tied-on chair covers, and fitted and draped tablecloths, to quilts and bedspreads, a padded headboard cover, bed skirt, and, of course, an inspiring collection of cushions to suit every room in your home. One word of advice: If you are a beginner, use step-by-step instructions literally – take it a step at a time, with the work laid out in front of you. Don't try to grasp all the techniques before you start!

Finally, I hope this book will be a source of practical ideas and techniques that encourages you to discover the versatile, exciting, and creative world of textiles for yourself.

Gina Moore 1997

ASSESSING YOUR FURNISHINGS

Seating

BEFORE MAKING cushions or covers, consider the shape and style of the chair or sofa, and how much wear it gets. Analyze the shape and style of the furniture – elegant, clean lines for a formal situation, such as a dining room; rounded shapes suitable for comfortable lounging; in-formal, collapsible chairs for outdoor use – and make a conscious decision to echo or complement this in your choice of cushion or cover. Then think about how the furniture is used, as this will influence the style of fabric you choose. A brocade or damask may be fine for a dining chair used only for special occasions, but a chair in a busy family kitchen, where sticky fingers and spilled milk are common occurrences, requires a sturdy, easy-care fabric that will stand up to wear and repeated laundering.

Dining chair ABOVE
Dining chairs have an elegant, simple shape. To complement this, try coverings that have clean lines, such as squab cushions (see pp. 68–71) and loose chair covers (see pp. 80–83).

Kitchen chair ABOVE
Kitchen chairs are generally plain and simple, and seat cushions should fit neatly so that they don't distract from their clean, simple lines. If the seat is already padded, a loose chair cover (see pp. 80–83) is the answer. For a kitchen chair with a hard seat, use a fitted squab cushion (see pp. 68–71), or make a box pillow (see pp. 72–75) to add extra height.

Wicker chair ABOVE
A fitted box pillow (see pp. 72–75) that molds itself to the form of a wicker chair provides comfort and a more luxurious look. To make the front of the seat look less angular, extend the pillow over the front of the chair and cover it with a rollover edge (see p. 75).

Director's chair RIGHT
Collapsible director's chairs are subject to wear and tear, and the seat and back can quickly get shabby looking. It is possible to replace them if you use strong chair canvas. Alternatively, stitch new fabric to the existing canvas or make a full-length cover. Try heavy, thick fabrics, such as velvet or tapestries, for a regal touch (see pp. 80–83).

Armchair ABOVE
An armchair, with its deep box-cushion seat and padded armrests, is designed for comfortable lounging and, as such, gets a lot of wear and tear. A drape (see pp. 84–87) is the best way to protect the upholstery. A simpler and less expensive alternative is a large throw (see pp. 88–91). If you don't need to cover the whole chair, a smaller throw, arranged over the back or arm, is a pleasing way to add color and warmth. Scatter pillows (see pp. 50–55) also add style and comfort.

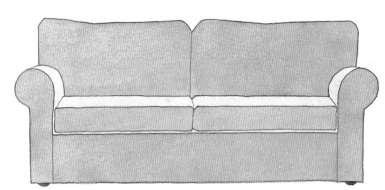

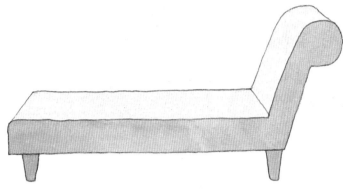

Sofa ABOVE

A sofa is often the focal point of the living room and should appear comfortable and stylish. To cover the sofa completely, a large throw is the simplest solution (see pp. 88–91). Sit separately covered box pillows on top of the throw to keep it in place (see pp. 72–75). A smaller throw that drapes across the back or arms can add color, warmth or glamour, depending on what fabric is used. If your sofa is deep and you need back support, make several large pillows to arrange across the back (see pp. 50–55, 64–67).

Chaise longue ABOVE

The rolled side of a chaise longue or day bed is an elegant shape that can be echoed by means of a rounded form, such as a bolster (see pp. 60–63). Another way of setting off the rolled side is to use a throw (see pp. 88–91) edged with a fringe or tassel, in a fabric that falls in soft but sophisticated folds.

Window seat RIGHT

A window seat is a neat, tailored shape that needs a cushion treatment to match. A button mattress (see pp. 76–79) with scatter pillows (see pp. 50–55) creates a comfortable sitting area. If the window seat is in an area that is not used much – a bedroom, for instance – a squab cushion (see pp. 68–71) will suffice.

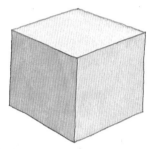

Lined foam block ABOVE

Make a box cushion on top for comfort, or a fitted cover on a firm cube of foam as a modern alternative (see p. 95). Covered in a children's fabric, the cube becomes a stool or oversized building block (see pp. 92–95).

Garden chair RIGHT

A collapsible garden chair benefits from the addition of color and form, and a squab cushion (see pp. 68–71) or a loose cover (see pp. 80–83) are both easy ways of achieving this. Make sure that the cover is easily removable and washable.

Bench RIGHT

Wooden or metal benches, both indoors and out, often need cushions to make them more comfortable. Fitted squab cushions (pp. 68–70) echo the neat, crisp lines of the seat.

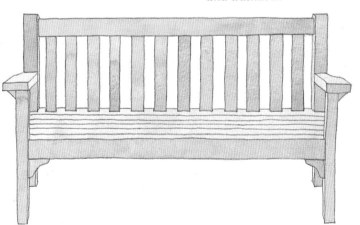

Beds

When choosing which type of bed cover to make, decide first whether you want a neat finish, with the cover tucked in so that the bed frame can be seen, or a more informal look, with the cover hanging over the edge of the bed and hiding the frame from view. In rooms where the bed doubles as a seat during the day, you might want to transform the bed with a lavish arrangement of throws and cushions.

Remember that items that need frequent laundering, such as quilt covers, should be made from easy-care fabrics.

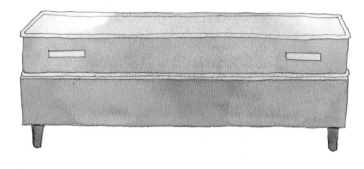

Divan bed LEFT
A divan bed has a low-profile, understated shape. In a teenager's bedroom or combination study-guest room where the bed becomes a sofa during the day, make two bolster pillows (see pp. 60–63), one for each end of the bed, and other pillows for against the wall (see pp. 50–59). Or, emphasize its real function with a fabric-covered headboard (see pp. 104–7) and a deep, comfortable arrangement of pillows, quilts, and covers. A sprung bed base can be hidden with a bed skirt (see pp. 100–103).

Child's, captain's, or bunk bed RIGHT
This type of box bed is suitable for either a tucked-in cover or an informal quilt or throw. A child's bed or bunk bed is usually given a simple treatment, with the focus on bright, cheerful colors, such as a patchwork quilt (see pp. 108–11).

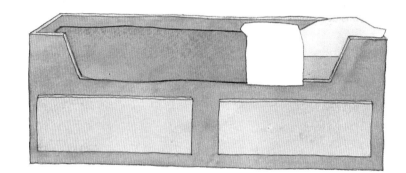

Bed frame BELOW
If you have a bed with an attractive frame that you want to show off, opt for a cover that tucks in, leaving the headboard, footboard, and legs visible. A bedspread with a fitted or shaped skirt is unsuitable for a bed with a footboard, although you can make a bed skirt (see pp. 100–103), adding a split in the skirt at the corners to fit around the legs or frame.

Futon ABOVE
When a futon doubles as a seat during the day, the prime concern is to have a cover that can be quickly unrolled and thrown over the bed in the evening. A throw, quilt cover, or throwover bedspread (see pp. 88–91) is ideal.

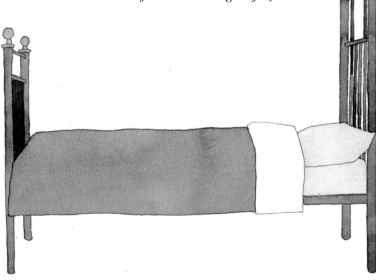

Tables

Before you make a tablecloth or cover, decide whether its primary function is to protect the table or simply to serve as a form of decoration. This affects the type of fabric you can use. For a dining room or kitchen tablecloth, where spillages are almost bound to happen and frequent laundering is essential, you will need a color-fast, preshrunk, stain- and wrinkle-resistant fabric. For a purely decorative tablecloth – in a living room or bedroom, for example – the choice of fabrics is limited only by your imagination.

Occasional table ABOVE

In a living room, an occasional table can be used as a practical place to deposit drinks glasses and trays, or as a display area for framed photographs, ornaments, lamps, and flowers. A living room table provides an opportunity to introduce color and texture to a room with a table cover that can be long and multilayered (see pp. 116–18). A long cloth can be protected with a more practical top cloth (see p. 119).

Bedside table ABOVE

Use a fitted cover (see pp. 120–23) to drape over a small table, shelf, or drawer unit to conceal storage space for bedside items. A loose, full-length tablecloth (see pp. 116–18) is another option. Choose fabric that creates a feeling of comfort and tranquility.

Dressing table ABOVE

A full-length cloth (see pp. 116–18) or fitted cover (see pp. 120–23) conceals extra storage space neatly. Choose fabrics that coordinate with other soft furnishings in the bedroom.

Dining table RIGHT

The same considerations for a kitchen table apply to a dining table. A polished wood dining table needs to be protected from heat and spilled liquids, so buy a heat-resistant undercloth and cover with a top cloth (see p. 117). For more formal entertaining, use a luxurious and glamorous fabric for the undercloth.

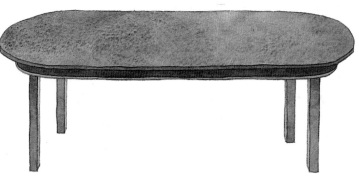

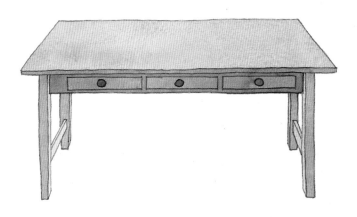

Kitchen table LEFT

The kitchen table is often the social hub of the household. Usually made with a wipe-clean, wooden or laminated surface, it can be transformed with decorative place mats or a tablecloth (see pp. 112–15). Look for easy-care materials or laminated fabrics, or have your own fabric laminated to coordinate all your soft furnishings.

ELEMENTS OF STYLE

CUSHIONS AND COVERS, bed covers, and tablecloths are used to accent or link other furnishings in a room. Choosing these items, and their associated fabrics, should be an integral part of choosing the style of decoration. If you are redecorating a room, consider cushions and covers alongside the wallcoverings, furnishings, and carpet. If you are working with an existing scheme, you will need to base your choice on features that are already installed.

The first thing to consider when decorating a room from scratch is your lifestyle and the function of the particular room you are preparing to tackle. You may, for instance, have a large family and require your main living areas to be practical and informal. But if you entertain business colleagues from time to time, you may prefer a more formal or stylish theme.

In most cases there are existing features, fittings, and furniture in a room that provide a basis from which to begin. An imposing period fireplace, a collection of strong contemporary art, or dominant floor-to-ceiling windows, for example, supply a focal point. On the other hand, negative aspects such as awkward proportions or an unsightly but necessary sofa, require solutions designed to divert the eye.

Usually you will have a color for walls already in mind, or carpet and upholstery already installed. You may have seen a piece of fabric that you have been wanting to use for some time. Use this as a starting point, and build other colors, patterns, textures, and trimmings around it.

Ask for samples of the carpet colors, wallcoverings, paint colors, and fabrics that catch your eye, then take them home and look at them in the room in question in daylight, at night, and by artificial light. You need to see fabric in as large an expanse as possible, so look at the fabric unrolled in the store and request a large sample. You can ask for a piece on a sale-or-return basis, or buy a small length that will do for a cushion later. It is far better to make the right decision at the outset rather than risk an expensive mistake.

Take all your samples with you when you shop. If you are working from an existing piece of furniture, can you remove a cushion cover to take with you? If you can't, and you have no swatches, try to match the colors using manufacturers' paint charts, or wool or embroidery silks, and take those with you.

Don't confine yourself to looking at furnishing fabrics alone. Cushions, particularly those that will receive little wear, provide a great opportunity to use dressmaking fabrics, but remember that these often come in narrower

***Easy styling* LEFT**
Scatter cushions can be used to lift a neutral scheme by adding extra color and texture. The use of stripes provides a link between areas of different color, in this case the cream sofa and deep red walls, while adding visual interest where there might otherwise be blocks of plain color.

widths. Look for period authenticity by visiting antique shops for old fabric remnants, lace, and trimmings. Then there are textile crafts such as patchwork, appliqué, embroidery, dyeing, stenciling, and printing. With these inspiring techniques you have an opportunity to produce your own combinations of color, pattern, and texture, adding a personal touch to a project.

Creating a sample board

Sample boards are used by interior designers to plan a decorating scheme. For personal purposes, you need only stick swatches in approximate position and proportion onto a sheet of paper. Start with the wall color covering a large part of the sheet, and use a spray adhesive that allows for repositioning to attach the other samples. If you don't have a large enough sample to keep things in proportion, substitute fabric or paper in the right color. Include samples of trimmings as, although they will inevitably be out of proportion, their impact is important.

The process will help you make confident decisions. Any tendency to play safe, particularly concerning large investments, will be more easily overcome because you will be able to build up a realistic picture of the effect you wish to create.

*A **sample board for a formal room*** BELOW
Deep colors and rich textures combine with elaborate trimmings for a warm and opulent setting.

Coordinating wallpaper links paint and carpet colors.

A deep burgundy adds warmth to the walls.

Plain velvet cushions add a soft, luxurious texture.

A tapestry fabric for armchairs, in a floral pattern that contains the three main colors of the scheme – burgundy, green, and cream – helps to link other areas of solid color.

A paisley design, rich in pattern and texture, drapes beautifully and makes a luxurious choice for curtains.

Rope and tassels emphasize the period feel and, by highlighting the three main colors, help integrate areas of color and pattern.

Satin brocade for cushions adds a smooth, light-reflecting texture to contrast with the heavy cut-pile damask on the sofa.

Chenille, matched to the color of the carpet, creates the correct proportion on the sample board.

A deep pile carpet in a warm neutral color works well with the dark gold in the fabrics.

Heavy damask has a rich, luxurious texture and is suitably hard-wearing for a sofa.

*A **sample board for an informal room*** BELOW
Soft colors and natural fabrics – both cotton and linen – combine with simple trimmings and sisal flooring for a cool, restful environment.

A cool tint for walls creates a relaxed mood.

Cream wallpaper with a tiny coordinating motif serves to lighten the room.

A bold ticking stripe for armchairs, plus ticking and natural linen for cushions, links the wall color with the natural unbleached color of curtains and trimmings.

Crisp linen trimmings for curtains and cushions emphasize a clean, natural look.

Unbleached muslin for lightweight curtains creates a feeling of movement and light.

Hessian, matched to color of the sisal, is used to create the correct proportion for the floor covering.

Natural sisal flooring adds a robust texture.

A floral upholstery-weight fabric for the sofa in softly faded tones ties in well with the sisal floor covering.

Plain cottons, in soft colors for cushions, coordinate.

CHOOSING COLORS

BALANCING COLORS IN a contrasting or harmonious scheme helps set the mood, and therefore style, of a room. For example, a selection of cool, airy pastels creates a sense of relaxation and space, whereas bright, rich primaries can be used to emphasize planes and angles, giving a feeling of vibrancy and contrast. The basic principles outlined below are intended to help you make confident color decisions that reflect your personal taste.

The color wheel

The color wheel is a valuable tool for decorating, helping you to combine colors successfully. Of course, it is unusual for color to be used in its purest primary hues, except perhaps for children's rooms. More often, subtler shades

and tones are chosen, created by mixing primary colors. You must decide whether to use a harmonious or a contrasting scheme. A harmonious scheme uses colors from the same side of the color wheel, or just one color. If you use a single color, work with different values of the same color, contrasted with a neutral color to avoid blandness.

A contrasting scheme uses colors from opposite sides of the color wheel. If the pure hues are used – reds with greens, blues with oranges, yellows with violets, and in equal quantities – the combination can be overstimulating and uncomfortable to live with. But when subtle colors are used, with more of one color than the other – a terra-cotta with sea green, for instance – the contrast can be what the eye seems to need to set off the dominant color.

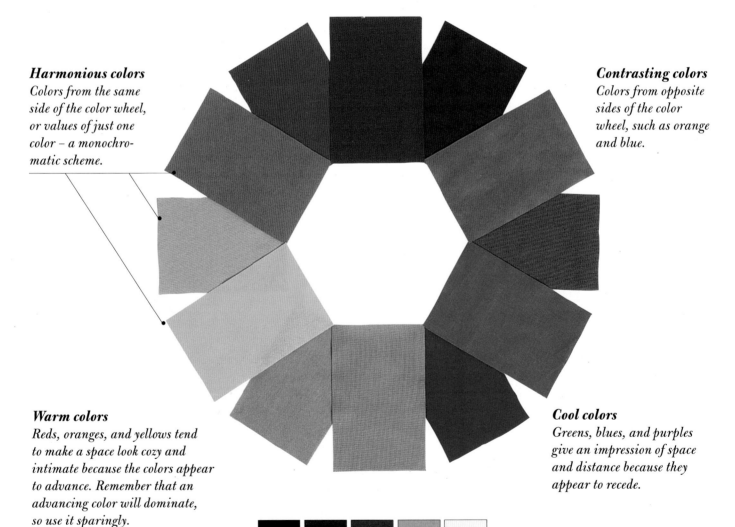

Harmonious colors
Colors from the same side of the color wheel, or values of just one color – a monochromatic scheme.

Contrasting colors
Colors from opposite sides of the color wheel, such as orange and blue.

Warm colors
Reds, oranges, and yellows tend to make a space look cozy and intimate because the colors appear to advance. Remember that an advancing color will dominate, so use it sparingly.

Cool colors
Greens, blues, and purples give an impression of space and distance because they appear to recede.

Monochromatic scheme
The simplest harmonious scheme is monochromatic, where a single color is used with different values of that color.

Neutrals and naturals

Neutral colors – black, white, and gray – are usually classed together, for decorating purposes, with the natural colors – cream, stone, sand, beige, and other off-white shades. Small quantities of black in accessories and detailing can sharpen a scheme more than any other color. The other neutrals are used as background colors in both harmonious and contrasting schemes and fabrics. Neutrals and naturals should be used with conviction, not just to play safe. Use them to provide a link between other colors and to tone down strong color schemes. They can be warm or cool, depending on which side of the color wheel they come from, and it is sometimes surprising how carefully they need to be color-matched. Neutrals and naturals can be used entirely on their own in a decorating scheme, often to stunning effect, but it is essential to provide contrast and variety in texture. Do this by building layers of texture using wood, stone, wicker, and sisal with unbleached canvas and calico, rough linens, and raw silks.

Neutrals: whites through gray to black

Naturals: beige, stone, oatmeal

Harmonious colors
A harmonious scheme creates, with the addition of neutrals, a relaxed, peaceful atmosphere. This works best in areas where you want to unwind, such as bedrooms and bathrooms.

Contrasting colors
Contrasting color schemes are lively and dynamic and are therefore good for kitchens and living rooms where social interaction is part of the room's function.

CHOOSING PATTERN

THERE IS A VAST CHOICE of decorative textiles, from rich, textural designs of tapestries and damasks to the printed figurative and floral patterns of chintz and the woven linear designs of plaids and stripes. Add to these the ethnic designs, such as Indian prints and kilim patterns, and more modern patterns inspired by contemporary artists, and the choice is limitless.

Textile manufacturers try to eliminate some of the angst involved in choosing fabrics by creating coordinating ranges available in several color schemes. A pattern, or part of a pattern, is reproduced on a different scale and echoed on borders and trimmings. Although using these ranges slavishly can look monotonous, many manufacturers work from a specific color palette, using the same shades across several ranges, making it easier to find fabrics that work well together without being rigidly coordinated.

What you choose will eventually come down to a matter of personal taste. The great thing to remember about cushions, throws, and covers is that they are a useful way of introducing areas of pattern to flat, plain schemes, or

Gingham check
Although this is a large gingham check woven in natural linen colors, it works as a subtle pattern. Like neutral colors, checks and stripes link well with other patterns and designs.

Narrow stripe
A very narrow stripe viewed from a distance can give an overall illusion of plain fabric. Used with other stripes, checks, and small prints, you can build stunning combinations.

Toile de Jouy
Toile de Jouy is a figurative design that originated in18th-century France. Although these fabrics depict detailed pastoral and mythological scenes, they are traditionally printed in pale blues and pinks on a white background and are a popular choice for bedrooms.

Abstract pattern
This modern abstract design works as a subtle pattern due to the distressed method of printing and the soft tone of brown on white.

Subtle patterns
Subtle patterns appear to recede. In small rooms they create space, but they can look insignificant in a larger area. They create a calm atmosphere suitable for bedrooms, bathrooms or any room in which you want to relax. Use subtle patterns in combination with other subtle and bold patterns to add richness and variety to the overall effect of a design scheme.

Small print
A small printed floral design is an excellent choice for small cushions, where its pattern will not seem insignificant. It works particularly well with checks and stripes.

Repeated pattern
A tiny woven repeated motif can lift an otherwise plain fabric and help to break up large areas, hence their frequent use for upholstery.

conversely, adding plain areas to a busy, patterned scheme. Putting different patterns together can be daunting, particularly if it is difficult to obtain large enough samples to see the effect. However, combining patterns is essential for a rich and varied decorating scheme, so some understanding of how patterns work together can help to simplify things.

Try combining patterns of a similar size. For example, a small gingham check might be placed alongside a small floral print. A strong design will marry with wide stripes, but use contrasting colors or the effect may be bland.

A bold pattern needs plain or small subtle patterns to break it up and prevent it from appearing too busy. Here, a restricted color range should be used.

Stripes and checks work a little like neutral colors, linking different designs and uniting patterned and plain areas. Plaids and multicolored stripes emphasize a color used elsewhere in a room, even if it is in the tiniest stripe.

It has become popular to put patterns together on one item – using checks and stripes to border florals and vice versa, and using techniques, such as patchwork and appliqué, to build pattern on pattern. Here the rule about keeping similar-sized patterns together is very important.

Large patterns can be wasteful as you must match the pattern across seams. Usually, large patterns work best on large items as you can fully appreciate the design. However, one large motif on a scatter cushion can look stunning, and is a good way to use leftover fabric.

Bold patterns

Bold patterns appear to advance. They make large areas appear more intimate and cozy, but can be overpowering in small rooms. Bold patterns create a stimulating atmosphere suitable for lively rooms such as the kitchen, but several bold patterns used together can create a busy, even disturbing impression. Contrast with blocks of plain colors for best effect.

Plaid
Plaids, like all stripes and checks, are extremely useful for pulling together disparate colors and patterns in a room.

Woven stripe
A bold multicolored woven stripe can be used alongside other strong designs in much the same way as neutral colors can be used with contrasting color schemes – to balance and unify a scheme.

Floral print
This floral print in a traditional pattern owes much to early Eastern influences in textile design. The bold and richly colored design is contained within stripes of subtle pattern, which makes it particularly suitable for use on cushions or other small items.

Figurative print
This bright figurative print takes its inspiration from India. It was divided into panels by a clever use of borders, which means it can be used on smaller items without interrupting the pattern.

Woven motif
A large woven motif in a strong color combination works well with other strong designs as long as the colors are harmonious (see pp. 14–15).

Ethnic print
This pattern is lifted directly from designs on carpets and kilims from the Middle East, where abstract patterns and symbols are an ancient art form. They are a popular theme in today's informal interiors.

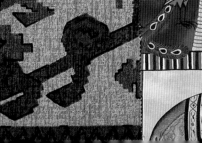

CHOOSING TEXTURE

TEXTURE HAS AN ENORMOUS bearing on the look and behavior of fabric, and must be considered alongside color and pattern when selecting material. Texture can affect our perception of color because of the way the surface texture of a fabric reflects or absorbs light. For instance, silk reflects light, making a color seem brighter and stronger. A fabric with a mat texture, such as canvas, absorbs light and makes a color appear darker and duller. Some fabrics both absorb and reflect light – for example, velvet has a deep pile that absorbs or reflects light, depending on the angle at which the light hits it. Richly textured fabrics, such as brocade, have a pattern defined by areas of shiny, light-reflective, satin weave against a mat, light-absorbing background.

Texture also affects the feel of a fabric. Smooth and sensuous velvets or fluid silks convey a different atmosphere from crisp cottons and tough canvases. Even at a distance, we know and respond to their differing textures.

Hessian
Stiff, scratchy, and unyielding, this fabric nevertheless has a place in today's natural, country-styled homes as cushion and table covers.

Indian hand-loomed cotton
This fabric has irregular ribs and an uneven texture for a pleasingly homespun look. It is suitable for all cushions and loose covers.

Corduroy
Corduroy is a hard-wearing, ribbed fabric that is soft to the touch – an excellent way of introducing a softer feel while maintaining a utilitarian function. It is strong enough for fitted cushions and loose covers.

Linen hopsack
This has a flat, slightly stiff but strong workmanlike quality.

Herringbone tweed
Made of raw silk, this fabric has a rough texture that belies a wonderful fluidity attributable to the silk content. A good choice for cushions and throws.

Informal fabrics
Informal fabrics have a harder, utilitarian texture for a practical, more contemporary look. These textures usually require the addition of equally practical-looking embellishments such as buttons and piping.

Canvas
With its tightly woven, even texture, canvas is extremely strong. It is useful wherever strength is a priority, such as for outdoor furniture or furniture in children's rooms.

Linen union
Another tightly woven, strong but plain fabric, linen union is traditionally used as an upholstery fabric, although it is also suitable for cushions and tablecloths.

The texture of a fabric is an important element of the way it drapes. Always consider the drape of a fabric for a throw or bedspread, as you need to ensure that the fabric "hangs" correctly and defines the shape of the sofa, bed, or chair you are covering. When buying fabric, test the drape in the store by allowing it to fall freely to the floor over a bench or chair – you will notice that the weight of a fabric can affect its drape.

Also, test the strength of the fabric – this is the firmness of the weave. The strength of a fabric can often indicate whether it is crisp enough to hold a pleat at the corner of a bed skirt, or pliable enough to be gathered successfully into a frill around a pillow.

The main thing to remember about using texture is the need for variety and contrast across all surfaces – floors, walls, and furniture. This will help you to create a well-balanced decorating scheme. This is extremely important in a neutral or monochromatic color scheme, where texture provides the only relief for the eye. Cushions and covers present an excellent opportunity for you to layer texture against texture. A linear room with hard angles can be softened with the luxurious textures of cushion fabric, or the suffocating atmosphere of heavy draped velvet in a living room can be lifted by adding a tablecloth of crisp linen to an occasional table, or shimmering, light-reflecting fabrics such as moiré or damask.

Formal fabrics

Formal fabrics are richly textured to create a luxurious, often period, feel. These textures are emphasized with traditional and elaborate ropes and tassels.

Chenille
Sometimes called poor man's velvet, this fabric has an uneven double-sided pile and a soft handle. It drapes well for throws.

Moleskin
This is a hard-wearing cotton fabric with a soft velvety pile. Good for fitted cushions and loose covers, where durability is important.

Indian dupion silk
This fabric has an uneven texture with a deep sheen. It is delicate, so is best for scatter cushions.

Velvet
The pile on this fabric runs in one direction. Run your hand over the fabric to feel which way it runs the smoothest. When light hits the velvet in the direction opposite from that in which the pile runs, it will absorb light and appear darker.

Damask
Damask has a complicated weave structure that uses contrasting textures rather than colors to produce elaborate patterns. Traditionally used for table linen, it is equally suitable for cushions and loose covers.

Cut velvet
Here, a soft, textured pattern is applied to a single-colored weave, adding textural interest to cushions and bolsters.

Crewel work
An embroidered surface pattern, often painstakingly hand-stitched in rich floral designs. It is very effective on bedspreads and cushions.

CHOOSING TRIMMINGS

Cushions

TRIMMINGS ADD AN ELEGANT and professional finish to soft furnishings, in the form of tassels, braids, and ropes from a *passementerie* supplier; buttons, ribbons, and lace from a haberdasher's; or piping, frills, and borders that you can make yourself using the same or contrasting fabric. They can define the shape of an item, while complementing the main fabric. The impact of, say, a tasseled cushion resting on the arm of a sofa is distinguished and theatrical.

When you shop for trimmings, always take your fabric with you; it is important to match both color and style. An elaborate tasseled fringe, for instance, would not suit a plain cotton fabric, while a simple cotton edging would look equally inappropriate on a luxurious velvet. You can use color in trimmings to accentuate a particular color in the pattern of your main fabric, which in turn helps to create a link with the other colors in your decorating scheme.

Also, think about your lifestyle. Decorative tassels are inadvisable if you keep pets, and dry-cleaning is a must for *passementerie*. However, trimmings do have a practical purpose – piping and braids add strength to seams and fabrics, whereas buttons and ties allow easy removal of covers when they need to be cleaned.

***Edgings* BELOW**
Pillow edgings, such as the flanged pillows shown here (see pp. 56–59), along with trimmings, such as piping, rope, fringes, or frills, create a visual outline for cushions and often help to reinforce seams. Some are inserted in the seam during construction, while others are applied afterward.

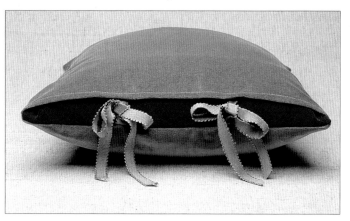

***Fastenings* ABOVE**
Instead of invisible zippers, use buttons and ties, ribbons and braids to fasten and decorate pillow openings. You can make your own covered buttons or search through markets for interesting buttons, toggles, or even beads.

***Corners* ABOVE**
Use tassels looped around rope edging, or tucked into the seams, to accent the corners of pillows. For a more restrained look, think of looping rope at the corners.

Bias-cut ticking
Bias-cut ties are a stylish means of fastening an envelope closing.

Matching piping
A slim line of piping in a shade similar to the one on the cover will accentuate the tones of the main fabric.

Braid and tassels
Braids admirably serve the purpose of covering the seams of cushions, while tassels are purely decorative details.

Wool cut fringe
A shaggy fringe works well with more substantial fabrics such as this heavy chenille.

Tasseled fringe
Rows of smaller tassels add a feeling of Eastern opulence, especially when they are in dark, rich colors and adorned with flecks of gold thread, as shown here.

Rope and tassels
Use a trimming in a strong, solid color to provide a sharp finish against a detailed and multicolored fabric.

Rope trimming
A coordinating rope trimming helps to bring out subtle areas of color, such as the narrow, colored stripes in this Jacquard check.

Cotton crocheted lace
You can use old pieces of fabric to make trimmings. Here, the lace from a damaged tablecloth contrasts well with the natural linen of this cushion.

Looped rope
Finish off rope edging at each corner with a double loop for a professional and individual finish.

Linen fan edging
A subtle, delicate trimming will daintily accent a pretty floral weave fabric.

Olive wood buttons
Wooden buttons look especially effective on country-style fabrics such as this blue gingham.

Pleated frill
A strong pattern can be edged with a contrasting color. Here the frill is edged and piped in a deep red, contrasting with the predominant blue of the plaid.

Throws, bedspreads, and tablecloths

THROWS, BEDSPREADS, AND TABLECLOTHS can be trimmed with flat fabric borders, fringes, braids, rope, and tassels, which are vital for defining the edges of usually flat expanses of fabric. They can also add weight to hems and corners, helping the fabric drape into heavy folds. Trimmings can create contrast in terms of color, pattern, or texture, complementing and linking to the other furnishings in a room.

SURFACE DECORATION

Surface embellishments provide a professional finish and add an individual touch to any project.

Tufts
Tufts are used to hold together layers of fabric and batting on a quilt or cushion, adding decorative effect. You can make them yourself from embroidery silks or wool (see p. 43).

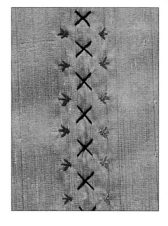

Embroidery
Although often deemed to be the preserve of the highly skilled, all you need is a few simple stitches and brightly colored silks to create stunning effects. Here, three rows of cross stitch create a border effect.

Double border
A double border gives a three-dimensional effect, creating a frame for the main fabric. Here, a printed floral cotton is edged with two plain linens for a bold finish.

Fan-edged fringe
The fan-edged top of the fringe softens the lines of a large-patterned fabric, such as this plaid moiré. The subtle variegated blues of the fringe also highlight the navy stripes of the plaid.

Deep linen fringe
A deep, lightweight linen fringe can emphasize the texture of the main fabric, here complementing the light and airy nature of a linen-print bedspread.

Self-piping and tassel
Adding simple, same-color piping and tassels to a rich fabric makes an elegant understatement. Here, the navy trim highlights the opulence of crushed velvet.

Multicolored border
Multicolored borders are perfect for patchwork projects. Here, colors that are dominant in the design are reflected in the border, adding to the vibrancy of the overall effect. For best results, use fabrics that are broadly similar in weight.

Bobble fringe
A bobble fringe adds detail to a bold-print fabric, such as this heavyweight plaid. The simple shape of the fringe has a naive quality that complements simple country styles.

Bullion fringe

A deep and heavy bullion fringe adds weight and formality to a floor-length circular tablecloth.

Appliqué

Appliqué is the application of a second layer of fabric onto a base cloth to create a pattern. The edges of the second layer are hemmed and hand stitched, or oversewn with a satin stitch. However, if as here you use a nonwoven fabric, such as felt, that does not fray, you can achieve almost instant results.

Buttons

Buttons are both functional and decorative. They are available ready-made or as a kit, ready to make yourself. For an indented effect, attach them in pairs, on each side of a pillow, for example, and pull them tightly together.

Deep border

Deep borders of fine or textured fabrics, such as satin or linen, make an ideal border for classic prints. Here, coordinating green linen edges a cotton-print throw.

Antique lace

An antique lace trim works best with traditional fabrics, such as cottons and linens.

Gimp braid

Gimp braid gives definition to the edges of fine fabrics, such as this silk taffeta throw.

Ornate tassel

A gilded wool and silk tassel adds weight to the corners of a tablecloth, pulling it into soft folds.

Rope border

A luxurious fabric, such as this floral red and gold Jacquard, can be edged with a heavy trim to maintain and highlight the richness of the fabric texture – here, a rope border is used to brilliant effect on a throw.

Shaped border

Zigzags and scallops add interest to a plain main fabric and are often used to edge short tablecloths, where the drape of the border can be shown to best effect.

CHOOSING PADS AND FILLINGS

PILLOW PADS ARE usually filled with a combination of down and feathers, or a synthetic fiber filling. Down and feather impart a soft shape and will puff up when "plumped" and filled with air. The higher the down percentage, the better. Buy pillow pads one size larger than your cover size for a plump, well-filled look.

For a firm-edged effect, choose a foam block cut to the required size and shape. Good-quality modern furniture often uses pillows with a foam core bonded to fiber outer layers, or wrapped in batting (see p. 33). For the best of both worlds, cover a foam core with close-weave, featherproof cotton stitched in channels and filled with down and feather.

Foam chips RIGHT
Although inexpensive, these make lumpy-looking cushions, but they are useful for floor cushions and outdoor cushions.

Polyurethane foam BELOW
Used for firm seat cushions, this can be covered with batting to soften edges (see p. 33). It is supplied in various thicknesses and densities, and cut to fit your furniture. It must be fire-retardant.

Polystyrene beads BELOW
This filling is used for bean bags. It must first be placed in an inner bag, usually made from cotton drill.

Polyester batting BELOW
Used for quilting and covering foam, polyester batting comes in various weights, from a thin 2 oz (57g) to a thick 12 oz (340g), and is sold by the yard (meter). You can also buy it in single, double, queen, and king-sized quilt sizes.

Polyester filling BELOW
Polyester filling is inexpensive and is sold by the bag. It is washable and non-allergenic.

Domette and bump BELOW

Domette and bump are woven, cotton and blanketlike interlinings used for nonsynthetic quilting. These fabrics are bought by the yard (meter) in various weights.

Pure goose down BELOW

Pure goose down is the best filling to use. Fine and fluffy, down pillows keep their shape for years.

How they compare
For a 20 in (50 cm) square cushion, approximate filling quantities are as follows:

Feathers	2 lb (900 g)
Foam chips	$1\frac{3}{4}$ lb (800 g)
Synthetic fiber or kapok	$1\frac{1}{2}$ lb (700 g)
Down	$\frac{3}{4}$ lb (340 g)

Cotton fillings BELOW

These are used in the manufacture of mattresses and futons. They are natural fibers, but will compress and become hard.

Down and feather BELOW

Available in various ratios of down to feather, the highest percentage of down indicates better quality.

Kapok BELOW

Kapok is a natural filling available in bags. It is very soft when new, but will compress and become lumpy over time.

Feather BELOW

The least fine and fluffy of the feather fillings, feather is widely used. It flattens over time and loses its ability to "plump up."

The Basic Techniques

MEASURING

T̲O MEASURE AND ESTIMATE fabric requirements for cushions and loose covers, first view your piece of furniture as a series of flat planes or rectangles that you wish to cover with fabric. Measure the dimensions of each one and add seam or hem allowances to all edges. For circular scatter pillows, for example, measure the width (diameter), and for square or rectangular pillows, measure the width, or width and length of the pillow, again adding seam allowances all around.

Estimating fabric

Because fabric widths vary, you cannot estimate how much fabric you will need for a project until you have selected your fabric. Always be sure to jot down the fabric width and pattern-repeat length when you ask for samples. To work out accurately how much fabric you will need, especially for more complicated covers, make a scale diagram the width of your chosen fabric and fit the pieces on it. Using graph paper will make this process much easier. Remember to allow for cutting elements, such as piping on the bias. As a rule, it is always better to over-estimate fabric requirements than to skimp and regret it later. You can always use leftover fabric to make smaller accessories afterward. However, bear in mind that covers for scatter pillows using a feather pad are usually made marginally smaller than the pad so that they look plump and full. For foam pads, make covers accurately to full size.

Seam allowances for the projects included in this book are all either ⅝ in (1.5 cm) or ¾ in (2 cm). If your fabric is thick or easily frayed, you may need to make your seam allowances wider. Thick fabric can create bulk, particularly at the corners, so you may need to trim seam allowances (see "Blunting corners," p. 36).

To estimate the length of piping required, measure around the outside edge of the pillow or piece that is to be piped (see the circumference labels on the diagrams below and p. 29) and then add extra for joining (specific fabric amounts are stated in the projects under

Measuring for seating

Bolster cushion
Measure around a bolster pad for the circumference, along the pad for the length, and across each end for the diameter. Add seam allowances all around. For a cover without a separate end piece, measure from the radius (half the diameter) of one end, down the length to the radius of the other end.

Fitted squab cushion and loose chair cover
For a fitted squab cushion you need to make a template of the chair seat. For a loose chair cover, measure all the surfaces you wish to cover with fabric and make a flat plan so that you can work out which edges need seam and hem allowances. For best results make a toile at least 2 in (5 cm) too big all around, then pin to fit on the chair.

Length of chair back

Chair back

Inside width of chair back

Length from top of back to bottom of skirt

Chair seat

Length

Width

Depth of skirt

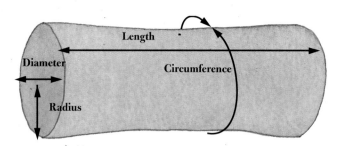

Length

Diameter

Circumference

Radius

"What You Will Need"). As a general rule, around 1 yd (90 cm) of fabric should yield 20 yd (18 m) of 2-in (5-cm) wide bias-cut strip.

Making templates and toiles

When you have to cut an unusual or complicated shape, such as a heart-shaped scatter pillow or a fitted squab cushion (see pp. 68–71), first make a full-scale paper template of the shape. If you are using a patterned fabric that you want to center on your cushion, a template allows you to move the pieces around on the fabric before cutting. Place it on the seat or cushion, and trace around the shape with a pencil. Lay it flat on a work surface and add seam allowances all around. Next, draw a pencil line down the center of the template. This will help you to place it on the straight grain, aligning it with the selvage (see p. 32, "Cutting on the grain"), and to center the pattern.

For loose covers, such as a loose chair cover (see pp. 80–83), first make a test cover, or toile, in a cheap fabric, such as calico. Make it loose to start, then fit it on the chair, making adjustments by pinning it and penciling new cutting lines onto the fabric. Make sure that it is still loose enough or that the fastenings are wide enough for the cover to be removed easily. When you've got it right, trim the fabric to within ⅝ in (1.5 cm) of the new cutting line, then use the calico as a template to cut the actual fabric.

Box pillows

You will need measurements for the width and length of the top of the cushion pad to cut the top and bottom section of the cover. Then measure the depth of the pillow and the length all around the pillow for the stand, or boxing strip. Add seam allowances all around. You will need to make a template of the top pillow if it is a more complicated shape, such as the horseshoe shape (below left).

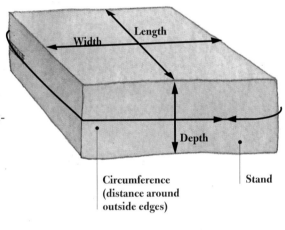

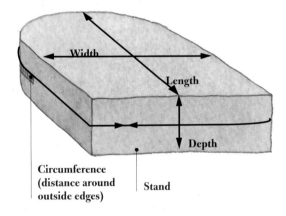

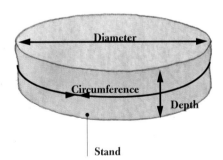

Sofa drape

For a full-length throwover drape, you will need two measurements: the measurement across the width of the sofa, from the floor on one side to the floor on the other side; and the measurement from the floor at the front, up and over to the floor at the back. If your sofa has separate seat and back pillows, you must decide before measuring whether you want your cover to go over them, or whether you are going to make separate box pillow covers (see pp. 72–75) to place on top.

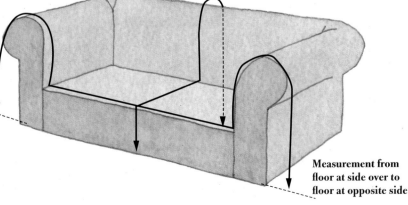

Measuring for beds

Headboard cover

To cover a headboard you will need to measure from the top of the mattress to the top of the headboard, taking the thickness of the headboard into account. To make a cover for a shaped headboard, you will need to make a template of the shape.

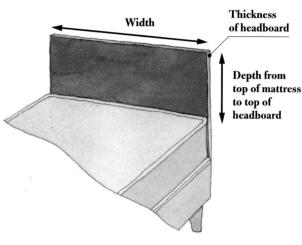

Bed cover

When measuring for bed covers, measure over the full complement of bedding, including pillows, and allow at least 6in (15cm) for pillow tuck-in. If the cover is to be tucked in around the mattress, allow 6in (15cm) on three sides of the cover to do so.

To estimate fabric quantity, allow for twice the length plus hem allowances, plus extra for matching a patterned fabric. Duvet covers are made to the exact size of the duvet so that they fit snugly. For a double duvet, you will need to join fabric widths to get the required width.

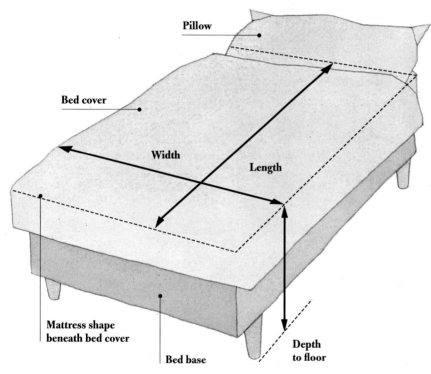

Bed skirt

The measurements necessary for a skirt are the length and width of the bed base and the depth from the top of the base to the floor. For the total length of the skirt, measure from 6in (15cm) in on both sides of the bed head (to secure the finished skirt on all sides), along each side, and around the foot of the bed. To allow for gathers, multiply this measurement by two. Cut widths of fabrics the depth of the skirt that, when joined, will equal the second measurement.

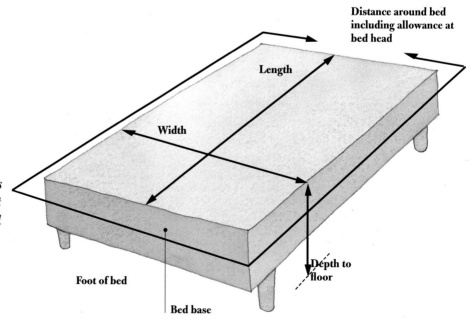

Measuring for tables

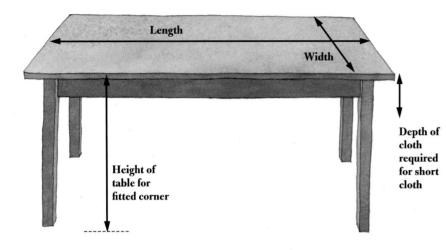

Length

Width

Depth of cloth required for short cloth

Height of table for fitted corner

Rectangular tablecloths
For rectangular tablecloths you need to measure the length and width of the tabletop. Then add twice the required depth of cloth. Measure from the tabletop to your lap for the maximum depth for a short cloth. For a long cloth, measure from the tabletop to just above the floor.

Circular and oval tablecloths
For a circular tablecloth measure the diameter of the tabletop, then add twice the required depth of cloth plus seam allowances. For an oval tablecloth, there will be a long and short diameter measurement. Add twice the required depth of cloth to both of these measurements, plus the seam allowances. To add a border you will need the circumference measurement (see the short bordered tablecloth, p. 119).

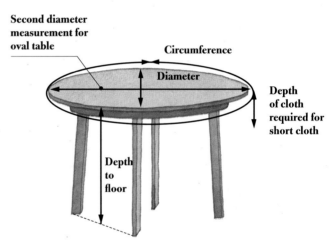

Second diameter measurement for oval table

Circumference

Diameter

Depth of cloth required for short cloth

Depth to floor

Estimating a pattern repeat

IF YOU ARE USING a patterned fabric, the design must match across the seams (see p. 36). This will affect your calculations for estimating quantities of fabric, particularly for large pieces such as bedspreads, throws, and tablecloths.

On some furnishing fabrics the size of the pattern repeat is noted on the label. If not, you simply measure the distance between the beginning of a design motif and the beginning of the next.

For smaller objects, such as pillows and chair covers, it is best to lay out your pattern pieces to estimate the fabric requirements. However, assistants in fabric stores will help you calculate your fabric needs.

1 *To work out amount of pattern repeats needed for each drop, divide size of the pattern repeat into the maximum length, or "drop," of your bedspread or tablecloth, including hems and seam allowances, and round up to the nearest whole number.*

For example:
Length of bedspread (94 in/239 cm)
÷ pattern repeat (12½ in/32 cm)
= amount of pattern repeats needed for each drop (7½ = 8)

2 *To find total amount of fabric required, work out length you need to allow for each drop by multiplying amount of pattern repeats needed for each drop by size of pattern repeat, and multiply this by number of drops needed.*

For example:
Amount of pattern repeats needed for each drop (8)
x size of pattern repeat (12½ in/32 cm)
= length needed for each drop (8 ft, 4 in/2.5 m)
x number of drops needed (2)
= amount of fabric required (16 ft, 8 in/5 m)

PREPARATION TECHNIQUES

Cutting on the grain

Fabric is usually cut on the firm horizontal and vertical grain – directly down or across the material.

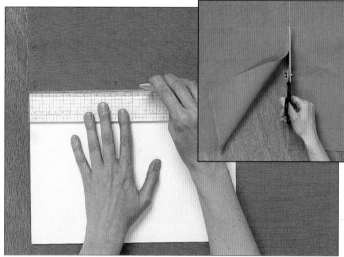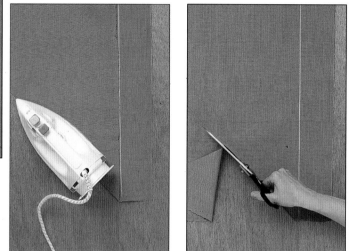

Place a sheet of paper along selvage to create a straight line at a right angle to selvage. Using tailor's chalk and a ruler, mark the cutting line along horizontal or vertical grain, or weave, of fabric. Turn fabric 90 degrees and cut along line (see inset).

Cutting on the bias

Fabric is cut on the bias when it needs to be flexible for borders or piping that stretches around curves and corners.

Mark the cutting line as for cutting on the grain (see left), then fold the fabric diagonally, bringing up bottom edge of the fabric to meet chalked line, and press (above left). Open out and cut along the pressed line (above right).

Cutting curves and circles

Use the method below to create neat, accurate curves and circles, such as the corner curves and quarter circles that are used on a bedspread or throw.

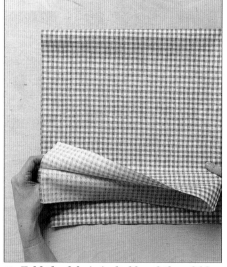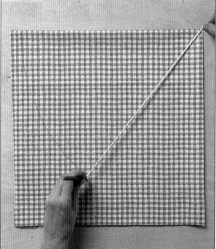

1 *Fold the fabric in half and then fold it over again so that you have four layers of fabric.*

2 *Cut a length of cord a little longer than the radius of the circle required. Hold one end at the corner of the folded fabric and attach the other to a pencil. With the string taut and the pencil upright, draw a quarter circle.*

3 *Carefully cut through all four layers of fabric along the pencil line. Finally, open out into a circle.*

Covering foam

Polyurethane foam needs to be covered with a lining to make it slide easily in and out of a removable cover. If your main fabric is not fire retardant, insert a fire-retardant liner fabric between the foam and the top cover.

1 *Cut a piece of lining fabric that is the size of the top and sides of your cushion with a ⅝ in (1.5 cm) seam allowance added on all sides.*

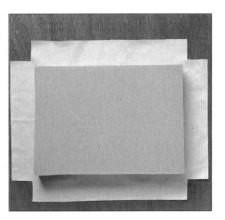

2 *Miter the four corners by folding the two short sides at each corner together with right sides facing and machine-stitch. Take a ⅝ in (1.5 cm) seam allowance and backstitch at the beginning and end.*

3 *Cut a piece of fabric to fit base of cushion, adding a ⅝ in (1.5 cm) seam allowance on all sides. With right sides together, machine-stitch bottom to top around three sides. Snip into seam allowance where fabric will turn the corner (see p. 37, Steps 1–3).*

4 *Insert the foam through the open fourth side. Pin the opening closed and slipstitch (see p. 34).*

Softening foam with batting

If you want to soften the shape of the foam, wrap the foam core with a layer of medium-weight polyester batting. Remember to take measurements for the cover fabric after you have applied the batting.

1 *Using the foam block as a guide, cut a piece of medium-weight polyester batting the size of the top and sides of the cushion with a ⅝ in (1.5 cm) seam allowance added on all sides. Miter each corner by drawing together the two short sides at each corner, and sew together by hand.*

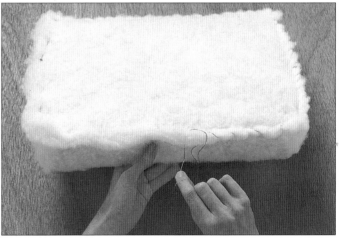

2 *Cut another piece of batting to fit the base of the foam, again with ⅝ in (1.5 cm) seam allowances added on all sides, and sew the edges by hand to finish.*

STITCHES AND SEAMS

Running stitch

This is a very short even stitch that you use for gathering fabric, such as for a frill border around a cushion.

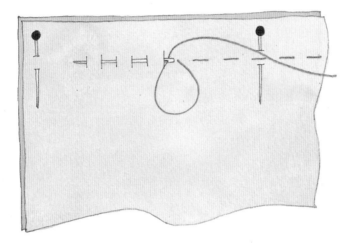

Working from right to left, weave the needle in and out of the fabric several times before pulling it through.

Even slipstitch

This is a nearly invisible stitch that you use to join together two folded edges.

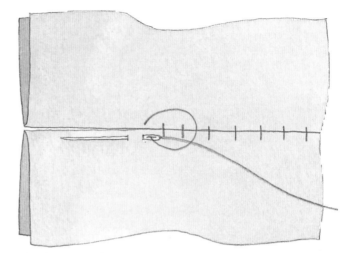

Working from right to left, come up through one folded edge and make a stitch about ¼ in (5 mm) long through the opposite folded edge. Pull thread through. Continue, making alternate stitches on each folded edge.

Uneven slipstitch

Also known as slipstitch hemming, this is a nearly invisible hemming technique that you use to join a folded edge to a flat surface.

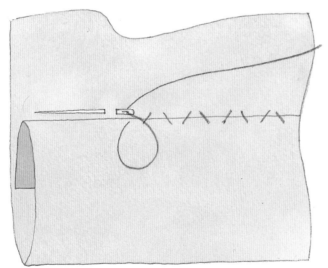

Working from right to left, come up through folded edge of hem. Make a small running stitch in the flat fabric, catching only a few threads. Make a ½ in (1 cm) running stitch through opposite folded edge. Repeat, alternating small and larger running stitches on flat fabric and folded edge.

Blanket stitch

Use this traditional embroidery stitch to provide a decorative touch around the edges of pillows, such as the flanged pillow (see pp. 56–58), throws, or bed covers.

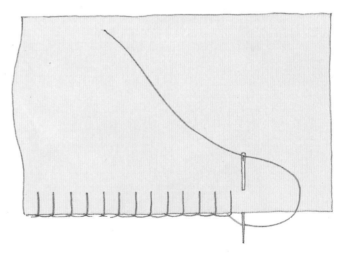

Working from left to right, secure thread and come up below edge of fabric. Go down into right side of fabric about ½ in (1 cm) in. Come up at edge, keeping thread from previous stitch under the point of the needle. Pull thread through slowly but not tightly, so that it lies along the edge of the fabric.

Sewing flat seams

A flat seam is one of the simplest ways to join fabric. To keep seam allowances even and seams straight, align the raw edges of the fabric to the appropriate seam guideline on your sewing machine.

1 *With right sides together, pin the fabric with raw edges and pattern, if any, aligned. Machine-stitch along the seamline. Backstitch at the start and finish of the seam to reinforce.*

2 *With right sides down, press open seam using tip of iron as shown. Turn to right side (see inset). Some seams need snipping before pressing to reduce bulk (see p. 37).*

Sewing French seams

A French seam is a self-enclosed seam where the raw edges of the seam allowance are sewn into the finished seam. Use it for visible seams, such as those on the back of an unlined bedspread, tablecloth, or throw, or for delicate fabrics that fray easily.

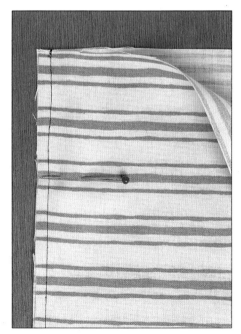

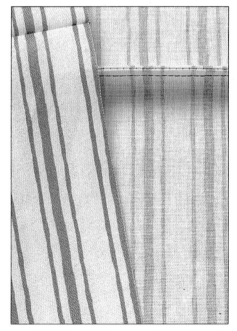

1 *With wrong sides together, stitch ½ in (1 cm) in from the raw edges. Trim the seam allowance close to the stitch line and press seam open.*

2 *Fold the fabric right sides together. Press again so that the stitched seam is exactly on the folded edge.*

3 *Machine-stitch a second seam, again ½ in (1 cm) from the stitched fold. To finish, press the seam to one side on the reverse so it lays flat against the fabric.*

Joining patterned fabric

Accurate pattern joining across seams gives a professional finish to your project. You will usually need to purchase extra fabric to allow for matching patterns (see p. 31).

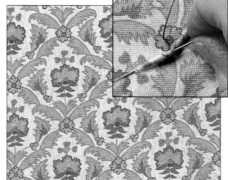

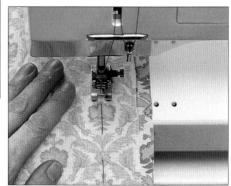

1 *Turn under the seam allowance along one edge and lay it over the other unfolded edge.*

2 *Match the fabrics exactly and pin in position. Use a big, even slip-stitch (see inset and p. 34) to baste the fabrics together along the folded edge.*

3 *Fold the fabric back so that right sides are together and machine-stitch the seam along the basted line of stitching before removing basting stitches.*

Blunting corners

Blunted corners create well-formed points when the fabric is turned right side out. Make one diagonal stitch across the corner for fine fabric, two for medium-weight fabric, and three or four for heavyweight fabric.

1 *Machine-stitch to corner, stopping just short of it. Lift foot and pivot fabric on needle. Drop foot and stitch across corner. Lift foot to pivot fabric before lowering and stitching in new direction.*

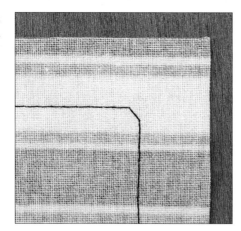

2 *To reduce bulk at corner of an enclosed seam, trim away seam allowance across the point, close to the stitching. Then taper on each side. Fabric that frays easily should not be trimmed too close to the seam.*

Snipping around curves

Snipping into the seam allowance of the straight piece of fabric allows it to lie smoothly around a curve. Use this technique when attaching piping to a curved seam, or joining a straight boxing strip to a curved section.

1 *Snip halfway into the seam allowance of the straight fabric where it is to join the curved fabric.*

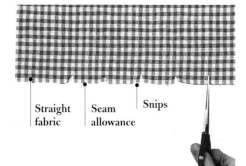

Straight fabric | Seam allowance | Snips

2 *Pin the two pieces of fabric, right sides together, ensuring fabric edges are aligned smoothly. Machine-stitch along seamline.*

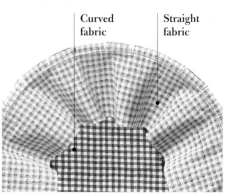

Curved fabric | Straight fabric

Snipping into corners

Snipping helps maneuver a straight piece of fabric around a corner – for example, when attaching a boxing strip to the flat top or bottom section of a cover, or fitting a straight run of piping around the corner of a cushion cover.

1 *Machine-stitch toward the corner, stopping about 1 in (2.5 cm) before it. Snip into seam allowance of top fabric where the fabric will turn the corner.*

2 *Continue stitching to corner and lift the foot. Spread the clipped section so straight edge fits around corner. Pivot work on needle so foot faces new direction.*

3 *Lower the foot and continue machine-stitching along the seamline.*

Finishing raw edges

Most fabric needs to be finished in some way to minimize the fraying of raw edges after the item has been made, particularly if it is something that will have to be washed frequently. Here are two methods.

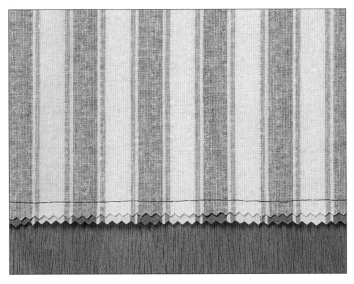

Pinking
Cut along the edges of seam allowances with pinking shears after you have made the cover. You can also layer the seam allowances to reduce bulk, as shown.

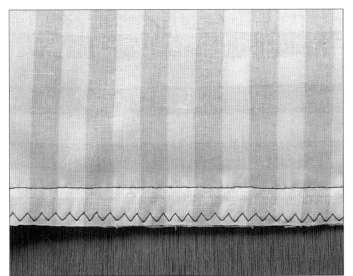

Zigzag stitching
Set the dial on your machine for medium stitch length and width. Stitch close to, but not on, the edge of seam allowance to stop fraying. You can use this on a single layer, or stitch two layers together at the same time.

BORDERS AND EMBELLISHMENTS
Making a double-sided miter

Mitering on one side of the fabric is generally used in hemstitching – see the fitted table cover (p. 120).
Use a double-sided miter to give a neat finish on both sides of the fabric. The width of the cut strips and
the seam allowance is dependent on the desired width of your finished border – here, 1 in (2.5 cm).

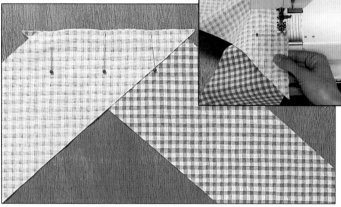

1 *Cut enough bias-cut strips to edge your border (see p. 40);
the width of the strips should be four times the width of the
finished border. Pin right sides together and machine-stitch,
taking ⅝ in (1.5 cm) seam allowance (see inset).*

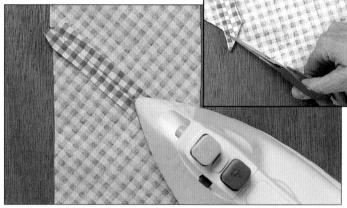

2 *Press open the seams and trim excess fabric at each side of
the strip (see inset).*

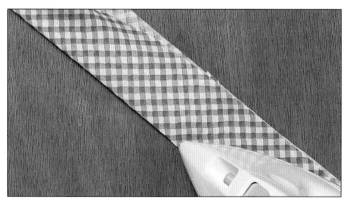

3 *Fold the joined strip in half lengthwise and press (this will
help you fold over the miter in Step 11). Open out the fold.*

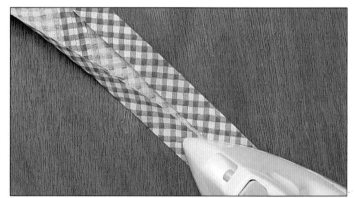

4 *Fold the two side edges together at the center, then press
along the length of the strip.*

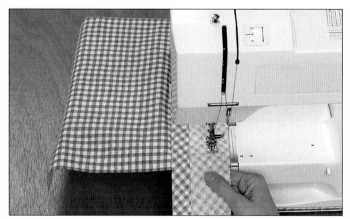

5 *Align the strip and main fabric, right sides together. Pin
and machine-stitch along the first foldline on the strip,
leaving the width of the seam allowance free at the top and
stopping at the seam allowance at bottom edge of main fabric.*

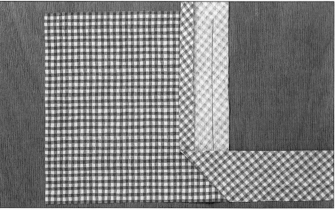

6 *Fold the strip away from the work at a right angle, making
a diagonal fold as shown.*

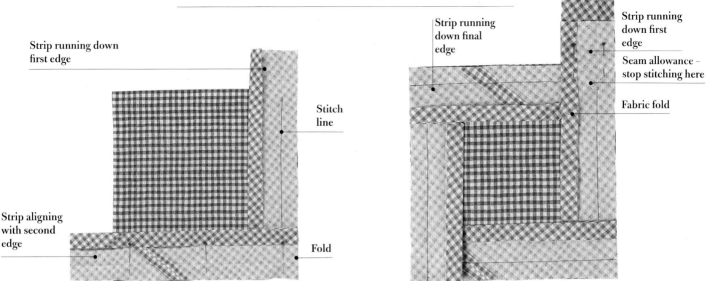

Strip running down first edge

Stitch line

Strip aligning with second edge

Fold

Strip running down final edge

Strip running down first edge

Seam allowance – stop stitching here

Fabric fold

7 *Fold strip back over itself toward the work, forming a fold that is aligned with next edge of the work. Pin and machine-stitch along line (see above). Repeat Steps 5, 6, and 7 along three sides.*

8 *At last corner, fold strip running down final edge as in Step 6 and stitch along strip up to seam allowance. Place strip running down first edge over strip running down last edge.*

9 *Turn the work over and machine-stitch over the border ends, close to the main fabric edge.*

10 *Using dressmaker's scissors, trim off excess fabric close to the stitch line.*

11 *Fold the border over the raw edges to wrong side of fabric. As you do so, a miter will form on the right side.*

12 *Turn the work over to wrong side. Bring folded edges of border up to the stitch line, forming a neat miter on wrong side. Pin in position.*

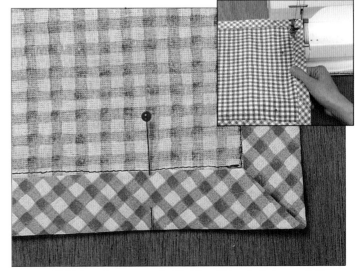

13 *Fold in miter around all sides. Slipstitch (see p. 34) along folded edge and miter, or turn to right side and topstitch by stitching through all thicknesses, very close to inner edge of border (see inset).*

Cutting and joining bias-cut strips

Fabric cut on the bias molds around shapes more easily, so use bias-cut strips to make ties and cover piping cord. They can be cut from the same fabric being used in the project or from a contrasting color or pattern.

1 *To cut bias-cut strips, fold over the whole width of fabric diagonally so the bottom edge of the fabric is lying along the selvage. Use a ruler and tailor's chalk to mark parallel lines, spacing them the width of one strip apart.*

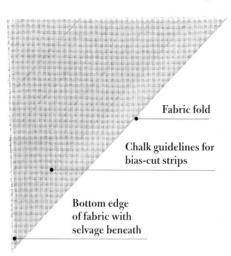

Fabric fold

Chalk guidelines for bias-cut strips

Bottom edge of fabric with selvage beneath

2 *Cut along the folded diagonal line and along all the subsequent parallel lines.*

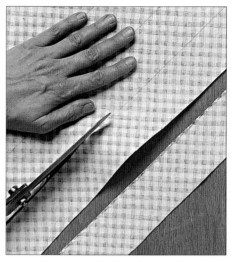

3 *To join the strips, pin the ends of two strips with right sides together and pattern, if any, matching. Machine-stitch ½ in (1 cm) in from the ends.*

4 *Press the seam open. To finish the strips, trim off excess fabric from seams (see inset).*

Making piping

You can buy cotton piping cord by the yard (meter) in many different thicknesses. For the majority of soft furnishing purposes, widths No. 3 and upward are normally used. Make sure that the piping cord is preshrunk.

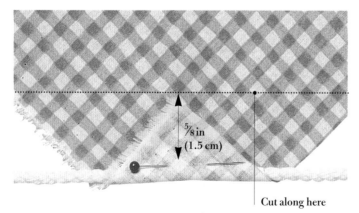

⅝ in (1.5 cm)

Cut along here

1 *To work out how wide your strips need to be, fold a corner of fabric over the piping cord and pin. Measure ⅝ in (1.5 cm) out from the pin – or ¾ in (2 cm) if that is the width of your seam allowance – and cut. Unpin and measure the total cut width. For other uses, such as ties, cut 2-in (5-cm) wide strips.*

2 *Follow Steps 1–4 above to make the bias-cut strips. Next, wrap the bias-cut strip around the piping cord, with right side out and raw edges meeting. Use a zipper foot on your machine to stitch close to the cord.*

Making rouleau ties

This method uses a tool similar to a long crochet hook, called a rouleau turner, to create rounded ties. If you don't have one, you can attach a large safety pin to one end of the loop and push it through to the other end.

1 *Cut bias-cut strips (see opposite) that are four times the finished width of the ties. Fold in half lengthwise with right sides together. Machine-stitch ½ in (1 cm) in from the folded edge.*

2 *Trim the seam allowance down to ¼ in (5 mm) from the stitch line. Trim accurately to this measurement to create an even finished shape for the tie.*

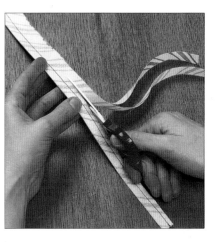

3 *Push the rouleau turner inside the tie and hook it to the other end. Carefully pull it back through, bringing the end of the tie with it until it is turned right side out.*

4 *To finish the end, simply tie one end into a simple knot and trim.*

Making folded ties

Folded ties give a flatter, more tailored effect than the rouleau technique shown above. Here, accurate pressing during the making of the ties is the key to a professional finish.

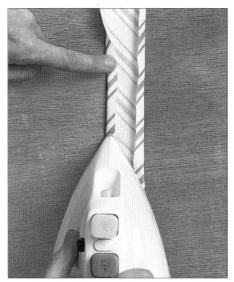

1 *Cut the bias-cut strips to the width required (see opposite) and press in ¼ in (5 mm) along each long edge of the bias-cut strip.*

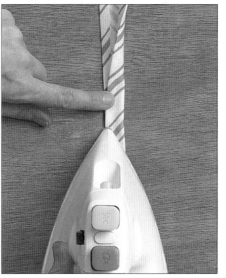

2 *Fold the strip in half lengthwise, aligning the folded edges. Press lightly, without pulling the fabric.*

3 *Fold in one end and stitch close to the folded edge. Pivot the needle at corner and stitch down the long edge as shown, again close to the folded edge.*

Making a self-faced frill

This technique for making a double-sided frill is suitable for projects, such as a pillowcase, using a light- to medium-weight fabric. If your fabric is heavyweight, make the gathering stitches by hand (see p. 34).

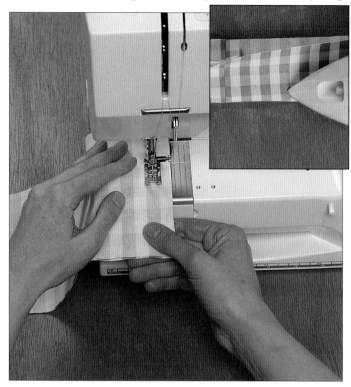

1 *To prepare the frill piece, cut strips that are twice the width and length of the frill you want plus two seam allowances. Machine-stitch side seams and press open, then press the whole frill piece in half lengthwise, aligning raw edges (see inset).*

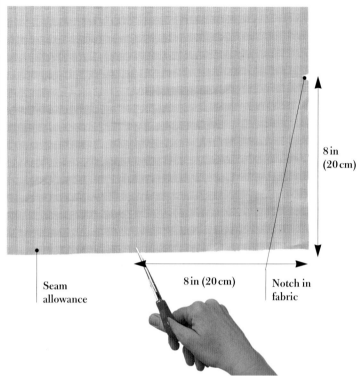

8 in (20 cm)

Seam allowance

8 in (20 cm)

Notch in fabric

2 *Take the main fabric and, starting from the corner, cut notches into the seam allowance all around at 8-in (20-cm) intervals as shown.*

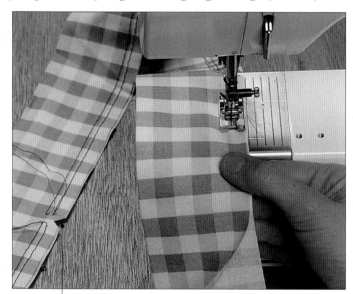

Notch along the length of the frill piece

3 *Make notches in the frill piece along its length at 16-in (40-cm) intervals. With a loose tension and a long stitch length, make two rows of machine stitching, one just above and one just below the stitch line of the frill piece, starting and stopping each row at a notch. Leave long thread ends.*

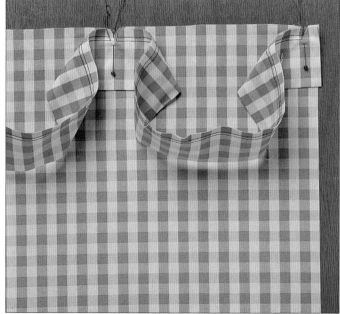

4 *Pin the frill piece to the right side of the main fabric, aligning notches on the frill with corners and notches on the pillow.*

| Figure eight around pin | Bottom row of stitching |

5 *Wind one end of the bobbin thread of each bottom row of stitching in a figure eight around a pin. Gently pull on the other end of the bobbin thread, moving the fabric along into gathers. When all the fabric is gathered, wind the other end of the bobbin thread in a figure eight around a pin. Repeat this process for the row above.*

6 *When the gathered edge matches the flat edge, even up the gathers and pin at frequent intervals. Make sure your machine is readjusted to normal tension before machine-stitching between the two rows of gathering stitches. Feed the fabric through the machine carefully to prevent the foot from pushing the gathers into little pleats.*

Making tufts

You can make tufts from tapestry yarn in a single color, or blend two or three yarn colors. Vary the thickness of the tuft as required – here we used 4-ply yarn, wound around the fingers eight times.

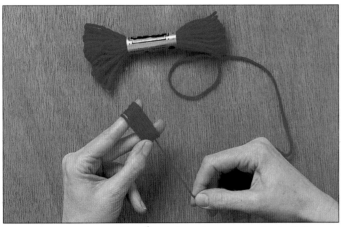

1 *Hold two fingers about ½ in (1 cm) apart and wind the wool around tightly. The thicker the wool, the less times you need to wind it around.*

2 *Carefully relax your fingers and slide them out without letting the tiny skein of wool fall apart. Wind the wool tightly around the center.*

3 *Tie off the end of the wool securely with a knot as shown.*

4 *Leave a long end of yarn with which to sew the finished tuft in place later.*

CLOSURES

Inserting a zipper

Zippers are inserted before the cushion or cover is made. Remember that if the fabric pattern is directional, place the zipper into the seam at the bottom of the cushion.

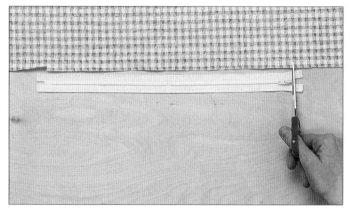

1 *Snip into seam allowances of top and bottom fabric to mark start and finish of zipper opening. Pin right sides together, aligning snips. Stitch from each snip to each side edge (see inset), ⅝ in (1.5 cm) from raw edge. Backstitch at both ends.*

2 *Machine-baste along zipper opening, right sides together. Break a stitch every 1 in (2.5 cm) with a stitch ripper to make it easier to unpick in Step 6. Press seam open (see inset).*

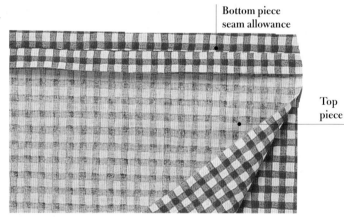

Bottom piece
seam allowance

Top
piece

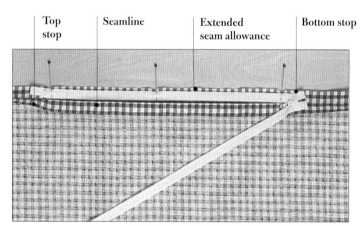

Top
stop · Seamline · Extended
seam allowance · Bottom stop

3 *Fold together the fabric at the stitch line, extending the seam allowance of the bottom piece of fabric.*

4 *With the zipper open, pin it face down with the teeth of the zipper close to the seamline and the top and bottom stops aligned with the top and bottom of the opening.*

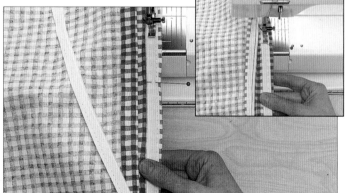

5 *Position needle to left of the zipper foot and machine-stitch in place close to the teeth. Backstitch at each end. Turn over the work and repeat Steps 4 and 5 for other side of zipper.*

6 *To finish, remove the machine basting using a stitch ripper and turn the work to the right side.*

Making a lapped zipper

A lapped zipper is hidden from sight by a fabric flap that disguises the zipper opening. To make a lapped zipper for a cushion cover, you will need two pieces of fabric for the back of the cover.

1 *Using the zipper as a guide, snip into seam allowances of the two bottom pieces of cover to mark zipper opening. Machine-stitch right sides together, from side edge to each notch, with a ¾-in (2-cm) seam allowance. Backstitch at both ends. Follow all instructions in Step 2 of Inserting a zipper (see p. 44) to baste along zipper opening.*

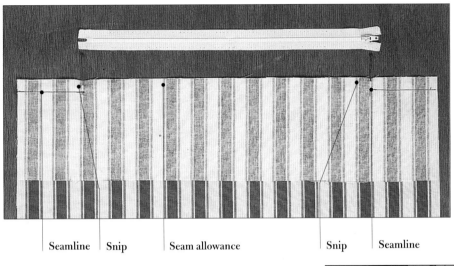

Seamline   Snip   Seam allowance   Snip   Seamline

2 *Open the zipper. Extend one seam allowance (see Step 3, opposite) and pin one edge of zipper face down on bottom piece, with zipper teeth along seamline. Using a zipper foot with the needle to the right of the foot, machine-baste in place about ¼ in (5 mm) from zipper teeth.*

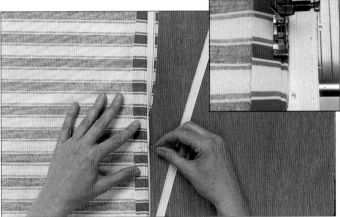

3 *Turn the zipper face up, tucking under the stitched side of the zipper. Machine-stitch very close to the edge of the fold, through all three thicknesses (see inset).*

4 *Turn the work around and extend the other seam allowance. With the zipper closed, machine-baste the other side of the zipper in place.*

5 *On right side and with needle to left of zipper foot, topstitch over bottom of zipper then along side of zipper, about ½ in (1 cm) in from seam, backstitching to secure. Repeat for top end of zipper.*

6 *To finish, remove the machine basting stitches holding the seam closed to reveal the zipper.*

Putting in a continuous zipper

Continuous zippers are used when the proposed zipper opening is long, for instance the back of a long seat cushion. You cut them to the length of the opening and then form the stops by oversewing the ends.

1 *Place the top and bottom fabrics right sides together. Cut a length of continuous zipper to the exact length of the opening as shown. Follow all the instructions in Step 2 of Inserting a zipper (see p. 44) to baste along zipper opening.*

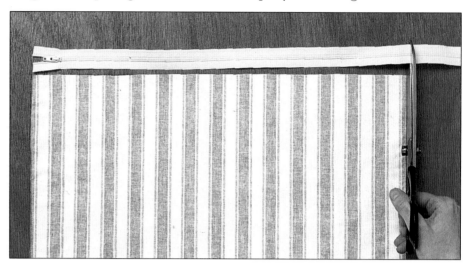

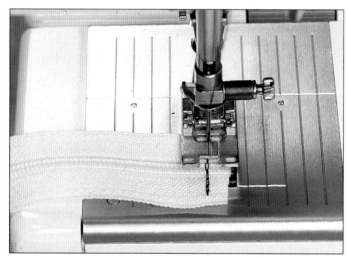

2 *Form a stop at each end of the zipper by sewing backward and forward several times across the zipper.*

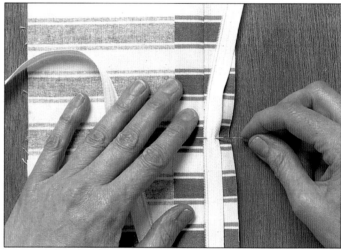

3 *Take the zipper opening and extend the seam allowance of the bottom piece of fabric (see Step 3, p. 44). Open the zipper and pin in position wrong side down, with the teeth lying along the fold line.*

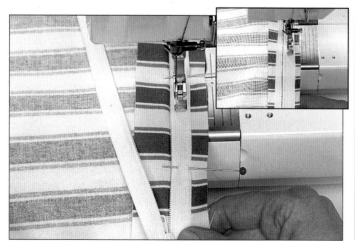

4 *Using a zipper foot, machine-stitch down the length of the zipper close to the teeth. Close the zipper and repeat Steps 3 and 4 (see inset).*

5 *To finish, unpick machine basting and topstitch over each end of the zipper to form stops (see inset).*

Making buttonholes

You can make buttonholes with the basic zigzag setting on a sewing machine. However, if your sewing machine has a special buttonhole attachment or program, follow the manufacturer's instructions.

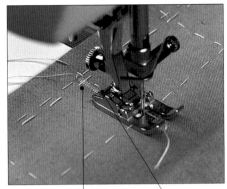

Beginning of | Center mark
zigzag stitching

Bar tack | Beginning of
zigzag stitching

1 *Mark the length and position of the buttonhole, using the button as a guide with rows of running stitch.*

2 *Set stitch width to medium, with needle set to left of center mark. Stitch down one side of buttonhole.*

3 *Raise the foot and pivot the work 180°. Take one stitch toward the outer edge. Take six wide stitches to form a bar tack.*

4 *Repeat Steps 2 and 3 to stitch up the other side of the buttonhole and make a bar tack at the other end. Set the stitch width to 0 and make three stitches.*

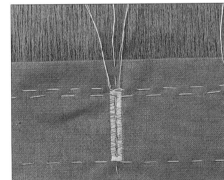

5 *Draw threads to the underside and trim. Remove markings and cut the buttonhole open using a stitch ripper.*

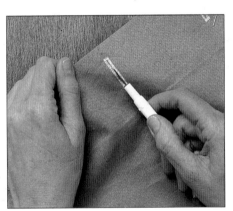

Covering buttons

The makings for covered buttons are bought in packets, usually with a front and back section for each button. Follow the manufacturer's instructions where they differ from those given here.

1 *Cut the fabric into circles about ½ in (1 cm) wider than the button top.*

2 *Put the button top into the center of the wrong side of the fabric and fold over the excess fabric, catching it on the teeth on the underside of the button. Use a pin to adjust the fabric uniformly around the button.*

3 *To finish, carefully push the back piece onto the button.*

THE PROJECTS

TRIMMED PILLOWS

TRIMMED PILLOWS ARE, quite simply, pillows with an additional decoration, usually sewn to the pillow edge. This is one of the easiest techniques to master, and collectively a variety of trimmings can create stunning effects.

You can plan a series of pillows that complement each other, and assemble them in groups at either end of your sofa or on easy chairs. Display tasseled and fringed pillows flat on the arm of a chair so that the trimmings drape over the cushion fabric, highlighting the contrast of texture and color.

Always make pillow covers slightly smaller than their feather pad so the pad is supported and firm rather than soft and formless. The main covers of all the pillows shown here are made from linen, but almost any fabric is suitable. When choosing fabric consider how durable it will need to be, and the style you want to create.

Pillow trimmings can match or contrast your color scheme, highlighting favorite shades or introducing new colors and textures to add subtlety and balance to a room. The four variations shown here include piping, rope trim, tassel fringe, and frills. Try piping and rope trim for a classic effect, frills for a country look, and tassel fringe for an ethnic look or simply a luxurious touch.

WHAT YOU WILL NEED
FOR A PIPED PILLOW

Fabrics

Main pieces
Two pieces each the pillow pad's width x the pillow pad's length (center the pattern if there is one)

Joined bias-cut strips
2-in (5-cm) bias-cut strips (see p. 40) to cover enough piping to go around all the edges plus 6 in (15 cm)

Accessories

Piping cord
Enough to go around all edges plus 6 in (15 cm)

Zipper
The length of one of the pillow pad's sides minus 4 in (10 cm)

Pillow pad

Piped pillow

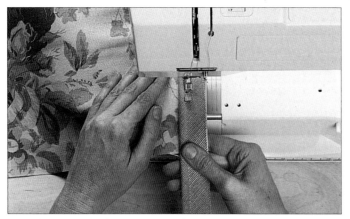

1 *Place top of pillow cover right side up. Lay piping (see p. 40 to make piping) along edge of one side of pillow cover top. With zipper foot pressed close to piping cord, begin to machine-stitch, leaving 1 in (2.5 cm) of piping free at the start.*

2 *As you approach the corner of the pillow, snip into the seam allowance of the piping so it opens to form a right angle. Blunt the corners by sewing a few stitches diagonally across them (see p. 36).*

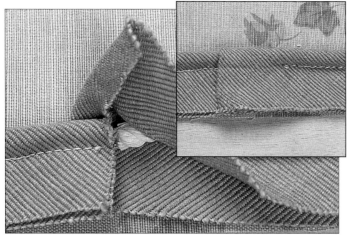

3 *Stitch around the cover, stopping within 2 in (5 cm) of the start. Unpick a few stitches holding the cord and trim it to meet the cord at the start. Trim fabric to ¾ in (2 cm), fold edge under ½ in (1 cm), and tuck under cord tail (see inset).*

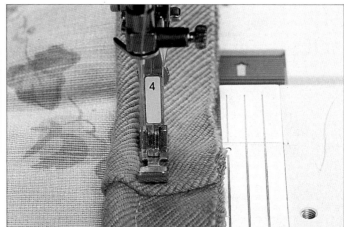

4 *Next, machine-stitch across the join in the piping cord as shown. Make backstitches at each end to hold the cord securely in place.*

5 *Insert the zipper in one side of the cover following the instructions on p. 44. Make sure that you insert the zipper along the bottom edge of the cover (this applies to all patterned fabrics that have a right side up).*

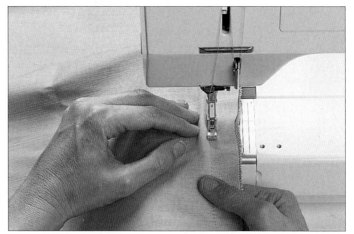

6 *Leaving the zipper open, machine-stitch the two main pieces together, again using the zipper foot pressed against the piping cord. Sew a couple of stitches diagonally across the corners to blunt them. Finally, trim corners of seam allowance, turn right side out, and insert pad.*

Pillow with rope trim

WHAT YOU WILL NEED

Follow list for Piped pillow on p. 50,
replacing piping cord with:

Rope
Enough to go round all edges plus 2 in (5 cm)

Key tassels
Four

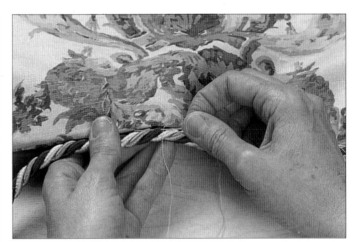

1 *Attach zipper to cover top and bottom (see p. 44), stitching together as in Step 5, p. 52. Stitch together sides as in Step 6, p. 52, leaving a ¾-in (2-cm) hole at one corner. Turn right side out and insert 1 in (2.5 cm) of the rope into the hole.*

2 *Hand-stitch the rope securely in place. Using strong sewing thread, sew rope to seamed edge of cover as shown with neat slipstitch (see p. 34).*

3 *As you approach a corner, wind hanging loop of the key tassel around the rope and secure with several hand stitches before slipstitching the rope around the corner.*

4 *At the final corner, wind the last key tassel in position and push end of rope into the hole, alongside starting end. Secure tassel and both ends of rope with hand stitching. For extra strength, turn the cover inside out and stitch together the two rope ends. Insert the pad.*

Pillow with tassel fringe trim

WHAT YOU WILL NEED

*Follow list for Piped pillow on p. 50,
replacing piping cord with:*

Tassel fringe

Enough to go round all edges plus 2 in (5 cm)

1 *Attach zipper to cover top and bottom (see p. 44), stitching together as in Step 5, p. 52. Turn cover right side out. Starting half-way along one edge, pin and slipstitch fringe in place.*

2 *Continue stitching to corner of cover, then fold fringe under and along the left-hand edge as shown.*

3 *Fold back fringe onto cover to form a miter. Slipstitch the miter in place and continue to pin and slipstitch along the fringe to next corner.*

4 *When you reach your starting point, cut fringe 1 in (2.5 cm) beyond it, tuck under ½ in (1 cm), and overlap one end over the other. Slipstitch down join as shown.*

5 *Turn over the work and slipstitch fringe in place, catching bottom edge of braid. Continue working around cover to complete. Insert the pad.*

Pillow with frilled trim

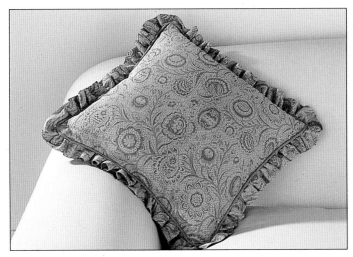

WHAT YOU WILL NEED

*Follow list for Piped pillow on p. 50.
In addition you will need:*

Frill

*Joined 4 ¾-in (12-cm) wide fabric strips, twice the outside
edge measurement of the cushion pad*

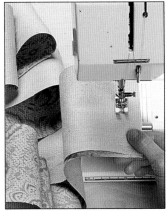

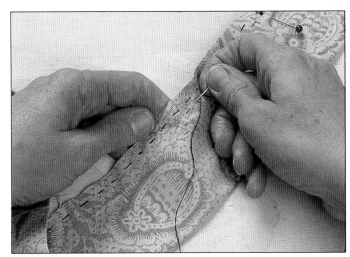

1 *Stitch together the narrow frill strips, right sides together, forming a ring twice the combined lengths of the pad's edges. Trim and press seams.*

2 *Fold in half lengthwise, press, and fold again. Divide frill into 8 sections widthwise by folding it in half, half again, and then half again. Mark folds by snipping into seam allowance.*

3 *Using strong sewing thread with a secure knot at one end, make running stitches ½ in (1 cm) from edge through both layers. Work left to right, starting at one end of a marked division and ending at the next. Then make a second row as shown, ¾ in (2 cm) from edge, working right to left.*

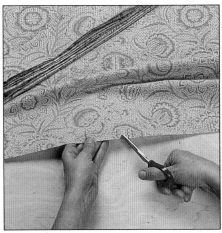

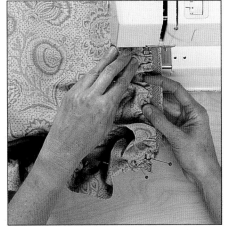

4 *Take the fabric for the cover top and mark the center of each side by snipping into it. This will help distribute frill gathers in Step 5.*

5 *Apply piping to cover top (see p. 52). Pin frill over piping, aligning raw edges and snips in frill to snips and cover corners. Pull threads at each section end, gathering fabric evenly to fit cover.*

6 *Wind thread ends around pins to secure. Machine-stitch frill to piped top, using a zipper foot. Insert zipper (see p. 44) and finish as shown in Step 6 on p. 52.*

FLANGED PILLOW

A FLANGED PILLOW COVER has a wide, flat self-border and is a simple and attractive way of using fabric to create something a little more out of the ordinary. Flanged cushions evoke a relaxed, country style. When placed casually on a wicker chair or stacked on a comfortable family sofa, the clean lines of this cover reflect a less formal way of living.

A "lapped" zipper is used for the opening: The back of the cushion is cut into two pieces and a zipper is inserted into the resulting seam (see p. 45).

Choose a fabric with body so that the flange is not too floppy. Look for a stiff organza rather than a soft voile, a crisp silk instead of a fluid satin, or, as we have chosen here, a ribbed cotton in preference to a listless, flat-woven cloth. The flat fabric border of this flanged cushion is the perfect ground for some exuberant but very easy embroidery stitches that complement the simple shape of the cover (see p. 58).

WHAT YOU WILL NEED

Fabrics

Top piece
The pillow pad's width plus 4 in (10 cm)
x the pillow pad's length plus 4 in (10 cm)

Bottom piece A
The pillow pad's width plus 4 in (10 cm) x a quarter
of the pillow pad's length plus 2¾ in (7 cm)

Bottom piece B
The pillow pad's width plus 4 in (10 cm) x three-quarters
of the pillow pad's length plus 2¾ in (7 cm)

Accessories

Embroidery silk
2 skeins

Zipper
The length of one of the pillow pad's
sides minus 4 in (10 cm)

Pillow pad

Making the flanged pillow

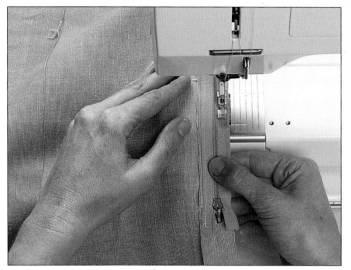

1 *Insert a lapped zipper (see p. 45) into the long side edges of bottom pieces A and B, centering the zipper.*

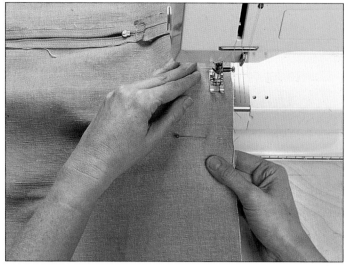

2 *Open the zipper and place the cover back on the cover front, right sides together. Machine-stitch around the outside edge of the cover, making a couple of stitches diagonally across the corners to blunt them (see p. 36).*

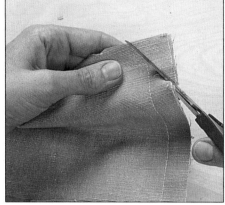

3 *Clip the corners by cutting away the fabric diagonally close to stitched seam, then turn pillow right side out and press.*

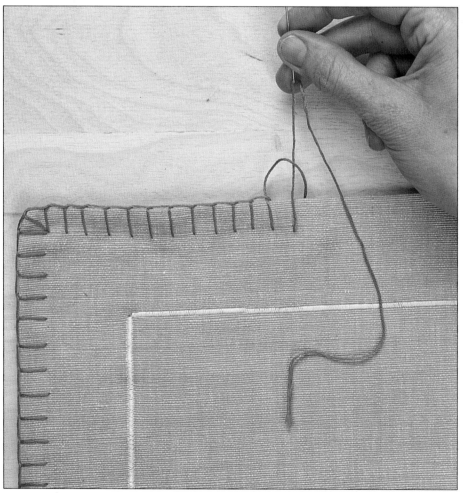

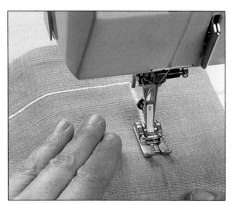

4 *Using a pencil, draw a line 2 in (5 cm) from outside edge all around the cover. Machine-stitch over pencil line with a narrow satin stitch, pivoting the work on the needle at the corners.*

5 *Finally, for a bold and decorative finish, use the embroidery silk to make large blanket stitches over outside edge of flange (see p. 34). Insert the pad and close zipper.*

FLANGED PILLOW WITH CONTRASTING BORDER

*For a variation on the flanged pillow, use a contrasting fabric
for the back and flange of the cover. This technique highlights the
flanged edge and emphasizes the soft shape of the pillow.*

WHAT YOU WILL NEED

Fabrics

Top piece
The pillow pad's width x the pillow pad's length

Bottom piece A
The pillow pad's width plus 8 in (20 cm) x a quarter of the
pillow pad's length plus 4 ¾ in (12 cm)

Bottom piece B
The pillow pad's width plus 8 in (20 cm) x three-quarters of
the pillow pad's length plus 4 ¾ in (12 cm)

Accessories

Pillow pad

Zipper
The length of one of the pillow pad's
sides minus 4 in (10 cm)

1 *Having inserted a lapped zipper (see p. 45) between bottom pieces A and B, press a ½-in (1-cm) fold around outside edge of this section, and then press a 2-in (5-cm) fold as shown.*

2 *Open out the second fold. Take the corner and fold it over toward the center until the diagonal fold line passes through the point where the pressed lines of the second fold intersect.*

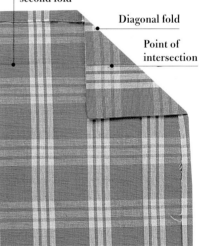

Pressed line of second fold

Diagonal fold

Point of intersection

3 *Refold the second fold as shown to form a neat diagonal seam at the corner. Slipstitch the diagonal seam in place. Repeat seam on each corner.*

4 *With wrong sides together, tuck raw edges of the front section under folded edges of the border and pin in place. To finish, machine-stitch through all thicknesses around the cover, close to the inside edge of the border.*

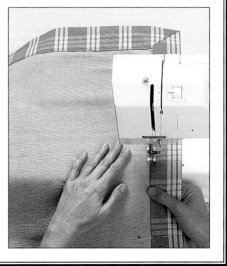

BOLSTER PILLOW

A BOLSTER IS A CYLINDRICAL pillow constructed from three fabric pieces. The main fabric is joined to form an open-ended cylinder, and two end pieces are attached to the main fabric, often gathered or tied to form decorative ends. The zipper is usually inserted in the seam of the open-ended cylinder.

A traditional place for a bolster is on a chaise longue, but more contemporary settings could be at each end of a bench, or nestled into the arms of a wide sofa. Made large, a bolster could span the head of a luxurious bed or form the cushioning at the back of a divan bed that is converted to seating use during the day.

Rich fabrics, such as velvets and silk brocades, used with lavish ropes and tassels emphasize the elegant period look of a bolster in a traditional setting. However, made in a striped ticking or simple gingham, a homely effect can be created. Here, eye-catching gold-print fabric was gathered at the bolster end to give an Eastern feel — a flamboyant contrast to the restrained elegance of the chaise longue.

WHAT YOU WILL NEED

Fabrics

Main piece
*The bolster's length plus 1¼ in (3 cm) x
the bolster's circumference plus 1¼ in (3 cm)*

End pieces
*Two pieces each the bolster's radius plus 1¼ in (3 cm) x
the bolster's circumference plus 1¼ in (3 cm)*

Fabric for buttons
Enough fabric to cover two buttons (see p. 47)

Joined bias-cut strips
*2-in (5-cm) bias-cut strips (see p. 40) to cover piping
twice as long as the bolster's circumference*

Accessories

Piping cord
Twice the bolster's circumference

Bolster pad

Zipper
The length of the bolster pad minus 4 in (10 cm)

Large self-covering buttons (see p. 47)
Two

Making the bolster

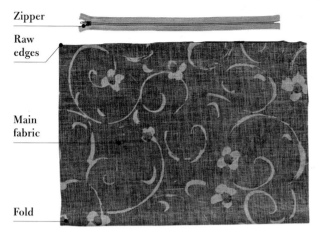

Zipper

Raw edges

Main fabric

Fold

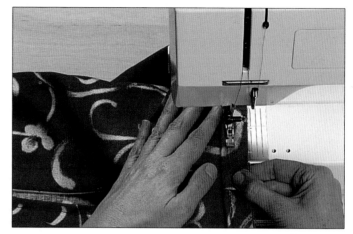

1 *With right sides together, fold main fabric in half so that the two shorter sides are together and pin. Stitch a lapped zipper (see p. 45) to the shorter sides, making a zipped cylinder.*

2 *Using a zipper foot, attach the piping (see p. 52) ⅝ in (1.5 cm) in at each end of zipped cylinder shape, starting and joining near the seam.*

Machine-stitch ends

Fabric is folded in half widthways

End piece

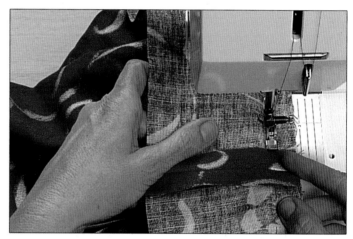

3 *Fold one end piece in half widthwise, right sides together. Taking a ⅝-in (1.5-cm) seam allowance, stitch ends to form a cylinder, backstitching to secure. Press seams open.*

4 *With right sides together and zipper open, stitch end pieces to each end of main fabric with zipper foot pressed up against piping.*

5 *Using a sewing needle and long length of doubled strong cotton thread, make a row of running stitches ½ in (1 cm) in at each end. Pull thread tightly to gather fabric in center. Secure by making a few stitches using gathering thread.*

6 *Make two covered buttons (see p. 47) and position over center gathers, one at each end of bolster. Stitch firmly in place and insert bolster pad through zippered opening to complete.*

BOLSTER WITH TIED ENDS

*There is no zipper in this bolster cover, so this bolster variation uses a contrast facing
on the inside of each tied end, with rope and tassels for added interest. You will need to undo the ropes and
gathering stitches at one end to remove the pad prior to cleaning.*

WHAT YOU WILL NEED

Fabrics

Main piece

The bolster's length plus diameter plus $13\frac{1}{4}$ in (33 cm) x
the bolster's circumference plus $1\frac{1}{4}$ in (3 cm)

Contrast facings

Two pieces each 8 in (20 cm) x the bolster's
circumference plus $1\frac{1}{4}$ in (3 cm)

Accessories

Bolster pad

Ties

Two lengths of tasseled rope, each 30 in (75 cm) long
(you can also use ready-made curtain tie-backs)

1 With right sides together, sew a contrast piece to each end of the main fabric, leaving a $\frac{5}{8}$-in (1.5-cm) seam allowance. Press seams open.

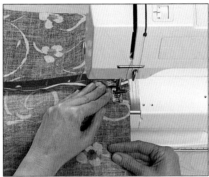

2 Fold in half lengthwise, right sides facing. Leaving a $\frac{5}{8}$-in (1.5-cm) seam allowance, stitch down the long side to make a cylinder.

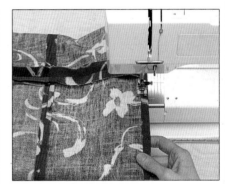

3 Make a $\frac{1}{2}$-in (1-cm) double hem on raw ends. Press contrast pieces along their seam line to wrong side of main fabric. Turn cylinder right side out.

4 Insert the pad and make a row of running stitches through both layers of fabric 6 in (15 cm) from the folded ends. Pull the stitches tightly to gather fabric.

5 Secure firmly by making a few stitches with the gathering thread.

6 To finish, wind the tasseled rope around the ends, covering the running stitches, and tie a secure knot.

TWO-TONED BUTTONED PILLOW

S AN ALTERNATIVE to concealing the opening of a pillow cover, you can make your fastenings the focus of the design. This buttoned pillow has a central cushion opening that is emphasized by brightly contrasting colors and large covered buttons.

Use this cushion where the detailing can be clearly seen. Place it on its own on an occasional chair rather than piled with others on a sofa. The strong colors need to be placed on a neutral background if they are not to fight with their surroundings.

Two contrasting plain velvets are used here to striking effect, although you can achieve a quieter result by using harmonious colors. Alternatively, use pattern to create contrast – a stripe with a check for instance, or a floral with a solid. Even more subtle would be to combine two fabrics with contrasting textures – a crisp linen with a smooth satin, or a nubbly tweed with a flat canvas.

WHAT YOU WILL NEED

Fabrics

Main fabric
The pillow pad's width x one and a half times the pillow pad's length

Contrast fabric
The pillow pad's width x half the pillow pad's length plus 2½in (6.5 cm)

Fabric for buttons
Enough contrast fabric to cover three buttons (see p. 47)

Accessories

Pillow pad

Self-covering buttons (see p.47)
Three

Making the buttoned pillow

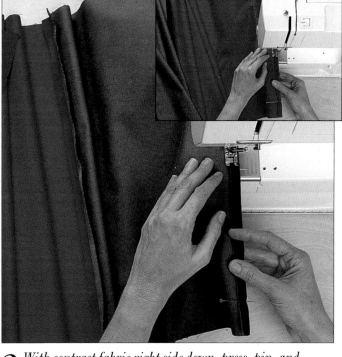

1 *Place contrast fabric on top of main fabric, right sides together, matching the edges. Pin, baste, and stitch along one side, ¾ in (2 cm) in. Press seam open.*

2 *With contrast fabric right side down, press, pin, and stitch a ½-in (1-cm) double hem along opposite edge. Repeat Step 2 along opposite edge of main fabric (see inset).*

Seamline

Contrast fabric

2-in (5-cm)
fold

Main fabric

Fold up
fabric to
center of
pillow

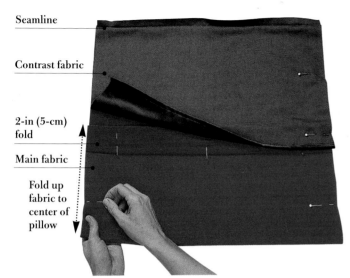

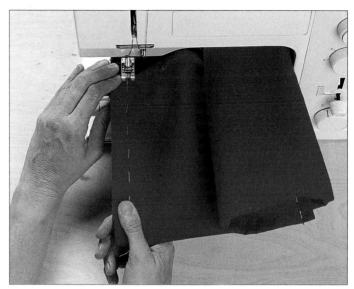

3 *Fold over and pin 2 in (5 cm) on doubled hemmed edge of main fabric. Take folded end of main fabric and, with right sides together, fold it up to center of pillow. Fold contrast fabric down from seam line and lay over top of main fabric so that both hemmed edges are aligned. Pin and then baste the side seams.*

4 *Taking a ¾-in (2-cm) seam allowance, machine-stitch both side seams (if you are using velvet you need to stitch these seams in the same direction). When you stitch the left-hand seam, neatly roll up the cover to get it under the arm of the sewing machine.*

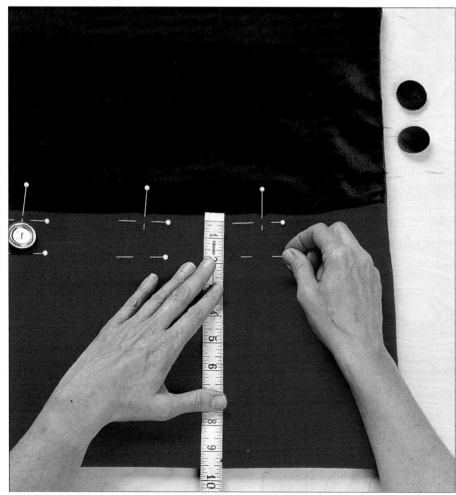

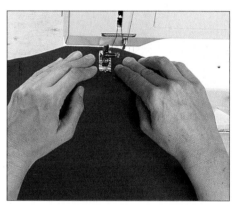

6 *Make the buttonholes using the buttonhole mechanism on your machine (see p. 47).*

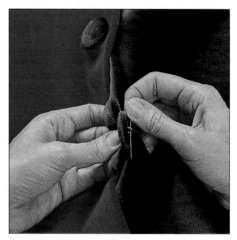

5 *Turn the cover right side out and, using one of the buttons as a guide for length, mark the positions for the buttonholes with pins or basting stitches.*

7 *Having covered the buttons (see p. 47), sew them on by hand, making sure that they are positioned directly beneath the buttonholes.*

PILLOW WITH TIED FASTENING

In place of buttons you could make a feature of the fastening with ties. Use these along one edge of the pillow and for added interest use a contrast fabric for the inside flap of the envelope opening. Here we used ribbon for the ties, but you could make them out of the main or contrast fabric (see p. 41).

WHAT YOU WILL NEED

Fabrics

Main fabric

The pillow pad's width x twice the pillow pad's length

Contrast fabric

The pillow pad's width x 6 in (15 cm)

Accessories

Ribbon ties

Four 15-in (38-cm) strips

Pillow pad

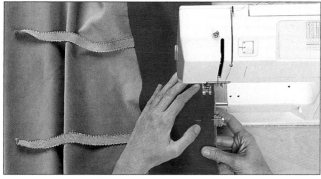

1 *Pin one piece of ribbon to right side of main fabric, one-third of the way along side that opens for pillow pad. Pin a second piece of ribbon two-thirds of the way along same side. With right sides together, lay contrast fabric on top and stitch along the side, catching ribbon ends in ⅝-in (1.5-cm) seam.*

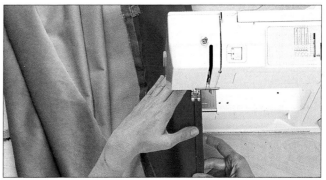

2 *Open sewn fabrics and lay down wrong side up. Turn over a ½-in (1-cm) double hem and machine-stitch along the edge of the contrast fabric that is opposite the one stitched in Step 1.*

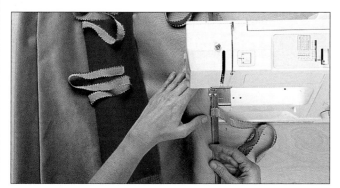

3 *At the opposite end of the main fabric to the one stitched in Step 1, turn in a ½-in (1-cm) double hem and tuck the other two ribbons into the hem, each ⅓ of the way in from the side. Machine-stitch the hem, stitching securely over the ribbons.*

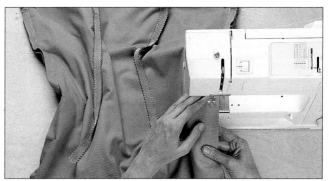

4 *With fabric face up, fold the double-hemmed edge of the main fabric to the seam. Fold the contrast fabric back from the seam over the main fabric. Pin, baste, and stitch side seams, leaving ⅝ in (1.5 cm) and turn right side out. Insert pad, tuck flap inside, and tie ribbons into bows.*

FITTED SQUAB CUSHION

HIS SQUAB CUSHION is tailor-made to fit the shape of your chair and is secured to the struts with fabric ties. It has coordinating piping and an overlap opening on the underside that makes it easy to remove the cushion pad, allowing you to change covers frequently. This is the ideal way to add padded comfort to upright wooden seats that look good, but don't feel it!

You will need to make a paper template for your chair seat, smoothing out tricky inside corners by cutting them as curves and adding a ⅝-in (1.5-cm) seam allowance all around. To make the bottom pieces, cut the template in two, one-third of the way down, and add 2 in (5 cm) to each cut edge for the overlap.

Bear in mind when choosing your fabric how often the cushions will be used. Fitted cushions usually get more wear than scatter cushions so it is important to use strong, closely woven fabric.

Bring color and pattern to your room by coordinating the cushions with a tablecloth or blind, or pick up on one of the main colors used in the room and use this as your inspiration.

WHAT YOU WILL NEED

Fabrics

Top piece
The chair seat's width plus 1¼ in (3 cm) x chair seat's length plus 1¼ in (3 cm)

Bottom piece A
The chair seat's width plus 1¼ in (3 cm) x two-thirds of the chair seat's length plus 3¼ in (8 cm)

Bottom piece B
The chair seat's width plus 1¼ in (3 cm) x one-third of the chair seat's length plus 3¼ in (8 cm)

Ties (x 4)
Four 4-in (10-cm) wide strips 18 in (45 cm) long

Joined bias-cut strips
2-in (5-cm) bias-cut strips (see p. 40) to cover enough piping to go around all of the edges plus 1 in (2.5 cm)

Accessories

Piping cord
Enough piping to go around all of the edges plus 6 in (15 cm)

1-in (2.5-cm) deep fire-retardant foam
Cut to the size of the chair seat (see p. 28)

Making the squab cushion

1 *Working with the wrong side of the fabric up, neaten the overlap edges of the two bottom sections by making double hems: fold over ¼ in (5 mm) and then another ½ in (1 cm) and press. Machine-stitch the hems (see inset).*

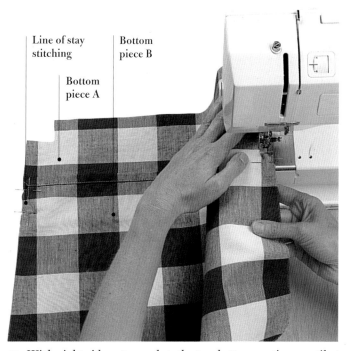

Line of stay stitching

Bottom piece B

Bottom piece A

2 *With right sides up, overlap the two bottom sections until together they correspond in size to the top section, and pin. Machine-stitch a line of stay stitching at each side of the overlap ½ in (1 cm) from the outside edge.*

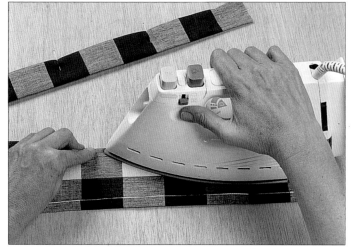

3 *Attach the piping (see p. 52) around the top piece. Start at the back, where the join will be less obtrusive, and clip and notch the piping seam allowance so that it fits around curves and corners. Snip the top piece's seam allowance at the corners and around curves.*

4 *Take the strips for the ties and press in a ½-in (1-cm) hem around three raw edges. Fold in half lengthwise and press.*

5 *Using the straight stitch foot, machine-stitch along the folded edges of each tie, keeping close to the edge.*

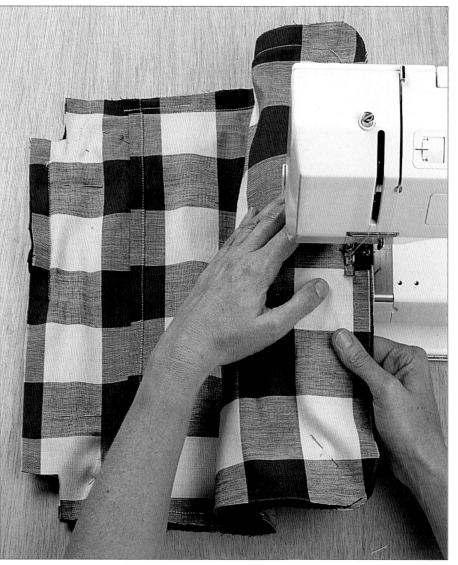

6 *Fold the ties in half lengthwise at the raw edge ends and pin to the seam allowance of the piped section on both sides of the inside corner. Machine-stitch back and forth over each end.*

7 *Pin the front to the back, right sides together. Using the zipper foot, stitch around outside edge, ensuring ties are out of the way. To finish, turn right side out and insert pad.*

ROUND SQUAB CUSHION

This squab variation shows how to adapt striped fabric to a round pillow. The center button obscures and strengthens the stress point where the segments meet. Because of this, the cover is permanent, so there is no zipper.

WHAT YOU WILL NEED

Fabric
One yard (90 cm) of striped fabric will be enough to cover most standard chairs.

Paper template for segments
Use chair seat to make a circular template

Fold template into eighths and cut out one segment

Ties
Four 4-in (10-cm) wide strips, each 18 in (45 cm) long

Joined bias-cut strips
2-in (5-cm) bias-cut strips (see p. 40) to cover enough piping to go around circumference plus 1 in (2.5 cm)

Accessories
Piping cord
Enough piping to go around all edges plus 6 in (15 cm)

Filling
To estimate filling, see pp. 24–25

Buttons
Two

1 *Pin paper template to right side of fabric (see inset). Draw a chalk line ⅝ in (1.5 cm) out from edges of template and cut out first fabric template. Discard the paper and use fabric segment as a template to cut out the other fifteen.*

2 *With right sides facing, and a ⅝-in (1.5-cm) seam allowance, stitch together the segments, matching stripes. Make two sets of four, and then stitch together. Repeat with remaining eight pieces. Attach piping to the top (see p. 52).*

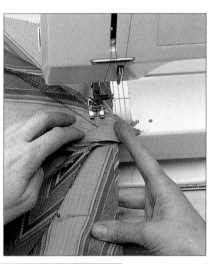

3 *Mark position for ties on back of bottom fabric circle. The ties should align with both sides of the chair uprights. Stitch them on and, with right sides together, pin and stitch bottom circle to top with a zipper foot. Turn right sides out.*

4 *Stuff with filling and hand-sew opening (inset). With a strong double thread, sew buttons on both sides of the pillow in the center. After taking one stitch through each button, tightly pull thread so buttons sink into pillow.*

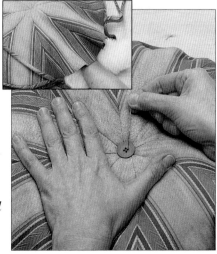

Box Pillow

A BOX PILLOW COVER consists of a top and a bottom section cut to the shape of the seat, plus a boxing strip to cover the sides of the pillow. A zipper is inserted into the boxing strip; here the zipper extends around the back corners, so an extra 6 in (15 cm) is added to the zipper length. The reinforced sides, or "stand," of the box pillow gives it its three-dimensional shape. This type of construction is used frequently for seat cushions on sofas, window seats, benches, and wicker chairs.

Since the places where a box cushion can be used are so varied, the choice of fabric is equally diverse. Bear in mind that seat-cushion fabric receives considerable wear, so your primary consideration should be the weight and strength of the fabric. Given that box pillows have defined form and are intended to reflect the shape of the furniture, closely woven fabrics are preferable.

Stripes and plaids need to be used with care, especially when matching the pattern down the front of the cushion. Center the pattern if there is one. Here, a strong, classic print in soft colors makes a striking contrast with the clean lines of the contemporary wicker chair.

WHAT YOU WILL NEED

Fabrics

Main pieces
Two pieces each the cushion pad's width plus $1\frac{1}{4}$ in (3 cm) x the cushion pad's length plus $1\frac{1}{4}$ in (3 cm)

Boxing strips
Two strips each the cushion pad's depth plus $1\frac{1}{4}$ in (3 cm) x the cushion pad's outside edges plus $1\frac{1}{4}$ in (3 cm) but minus the zipper's length, cut into two equal lengths

Zipper strips
Two strips each half the cushion pad's depth plus $1\frac{1}{4}$ in (3 cm) x the zipper's length plus $1\frac{1}{4}$ in (3 cm)

Joined bias-cut strips
2-in (5-cm) bias-cut strips (see p. 40) to cover enough piping to go around all edges twice plus 1 in (2.5 cm)

Accessories

Piping cord
Enough to go around all edges twice plus 6 in (15 cm)

Continuous zipper
The length of cushion's back edge plus 6 in (15 cm)

Cushion pad

Making the box pillow

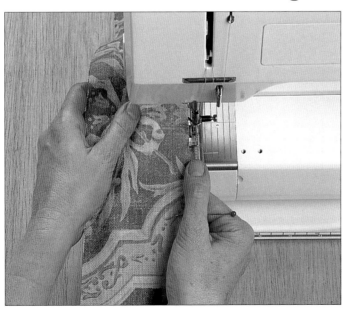

1 *Press under a ⅝-in (1.5-cm) seam allowance along one longer edge of both of the zipper strips.*

2 *With the strip right side up, place one side of zipper under pressed edge of fabric so that zipper tape is completely covered and zipper teeth are close against the edge. Machine-stitch using a zipper foot as shown.*

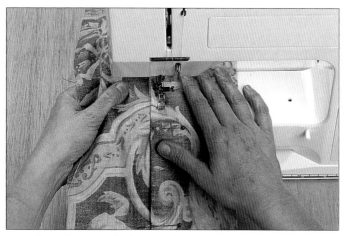

3 *Close zipper and pin second strip to its other side, so that pressed fabric edge meets opposite folded edge of the first strip and covers zipper teeth. Again, machine-stitch using zipper foot as shown.*

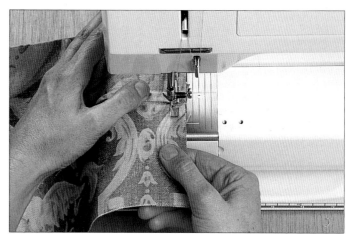

4 *Oversew each end of the zipper (see p. 46) by machine-stitching backwards and forwards over the ends ½ in (1 cm) from the end of the fabric. The stitches are then within the ⅝-in (1.5-cm) seam allowance.*

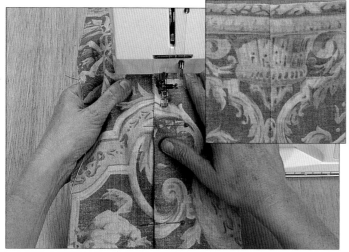

5 *Stitch together the other strips of fabric that make up the boxing strip and attach the zipper strip to both ends, making a ring. Match the pattern of your fabric so that the design reads across the seam (see inset and p. 36).*

6 *Machine-stitch piping (see p. 52) to top and bottom of the stand using a zipper foot and leaving a ⅝-in (1.5-cm) seam allowance. Start and finish both rows at back of cushion by the zipper so that the joins are unobtrusive.*

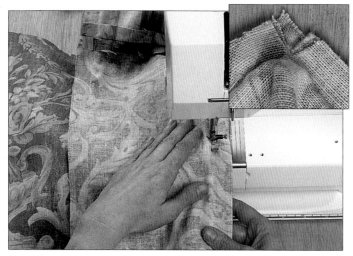

7 *With right sides together, pin and stitch bottom piece of cover to bottom edge of piped stand, making sure zipper is placed centrally at back. Snip seam allowance of piping and stand so that it fits around corners of the cushion (see inset).*

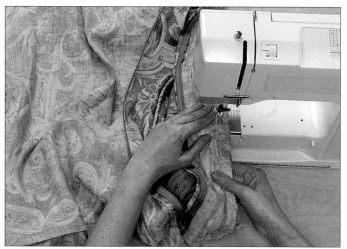

8 *Repeat Step 7 to attach top of cover to top edge of piped stand, leaving zipper undone so that you can turn cover right side out when you are finished. Turn cover right side out and insert pad.*

BOX PILLOW WITH ROLLOVER FRONT EDGE

This box cushion is especially suitable for a striped or plaid fabric. Cut the top, bottom, and front fabric as one piece. Curve the corners at both ends of the remaining stand so that the fabric rolls over at the front of the cushion.

WHAT YOU WILL NEED

Fabrics

Main piece

The cushion pad's width plus $1\frac{1}{4}$ in (3 cm) x twice the cushion pad's length plus the depth plus $1\frac{1}{4}$ in (3 cm)

Boxing strip

The cushion pad's depth plus $1\frac{1}{4}$ in (3 cm) x the cushion pad's sides plus back plus $1\frac{1}{4}$ in (3 cm) but minus the zipper's length

Zipper strips

Two strips each half the cushion pad's depth plus $1\frac{1}{4}$ in (3 cm) x the zipper's length plus $1\frac{1}{4}$ in (3 cm)

Joined bias-cut strips

2-in (5-cm) bias-cut strips (see p. 40) to cover enough piping to go around all edges twice plus 1 in (2.5 cm)

Accessories

Piping cord

Enough to go around all edges twice plus 6 in (15 cm)

Continuous zipper

The length of cushion's back edge plus 6 in (15 cm)

Cushion pad

1 *Follow Steps 1–4 (pp. 73–74) to insert zipper into the zipper strips and stitch the boxing strips to both ends of the zipper section. Fold it in half lengthwise and, using a saucer as a template, draw a curve for each front corner. Cut around curved lines.*

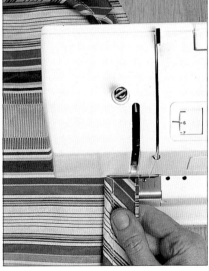

2 *Attach the covered piping (see p. 52) around the boxing strip, starting by the zipper. Continue around the curved front corners, clipping the allowances to ease them around the curves. Join the piping.*

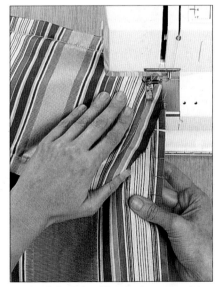

3 *With right sides facing, pin the boxing strip to the main section, centering the zipper across the back. Stitch using a zipper foot, snipping the seam allowance to ease it around the curved corners. Turn the cushion right side out and insert the pad.*

BUTTON MATTRESS

THIS CUSHION IS BASED on the design of a traditional mattress that would have been stuffed with cotton or kapok batting. Here we used a foam cushion wrapped in the thickest kind of polyester batting to give it a soft outline. The boxing strip around the sides is quilted with the batting and muslin with vertical rows of machine stitching. Thick wadded pleats were made along the top and bottom to create the welt along the edges. The buttons add a purely decorative touch. The cover is not removable, so there is no need for a zipper or other fastening on the mattress.

Typically, this type of mattress suits stools of all shapes and sizes. However, you can adapt it to add comfort to a hard wooden bench or old blanket chest, to provide padding on a window seat, or to serve as a stylish mattress for a wrought-iron day bed.

The fabric used here is traditional ticking, a tightly woven and robust herringbone cotton. However, any striped fabric works well as long as it is reasonably sturdy. Alternatively, you could use a plain fabric, such as a natural canvas, or a brightly colored sailcloth set off with buttons or tufts in a contrasting color.

WHAT YOU WILL NEED

Fabric

Top and bottom cover
Two pieces, each the cushion's width plus 1½ in (4 cm) x the cushion's length plus 1½ in (4 cm)

Boxing strip
Joined strips of fabric measuring the cushion's depth plus 6½ in (16 cm) x the cushion's outside edges plus 1½ in (4 cm)

Fabric for buttons
Enough fabric to cover sixteen buttons (see p. 47)

Accessories

Batting
Enough to wrap up the foam pad, plus side strips totaling the cushion's depth plus 4 in (10 cm) x the cushion's outside edges

Muslin
Strips of muslin totaling the cushion's depth plus 5½ in (14 cm) x the cushion's outside edges plus 1½ in (4 cm)

Foam pad
The size of the finished cushion minus 1½ in (4 cm) from the length, width, and depth

Spray adhesive

Self-covering buttons
Sixteen

Mattress needle

Button thread

Making the mattress

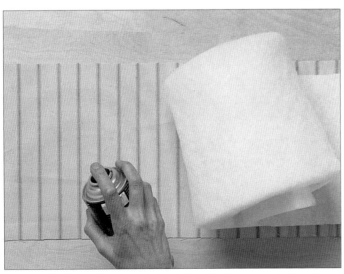

1 Lay the joined boxing strip right side down, and place the batting strips on top of it. There should be ¾ in (2 cm) of fabric showing at the top and bottom and at each end. Use a light coating of spray adhesive to fix the batting in place on the fabric.

2 Fix the muslin strips over the batting with the adhesive in the same way. (The muslin makes the boxing strip easier to machine-quilt – the batting won't get caught in the feed dog of the machine and will stay in place better.)

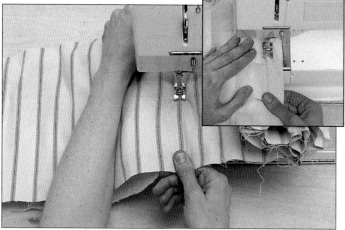

3 *With the strip right side up, machine-stitch vertical rows at 2-in (5-cm) intervals along boxing strip. Then stitch together the two ends of the strip – right sides together, ¾ in (2 cm) from the edge – to form a ring (see inset).*

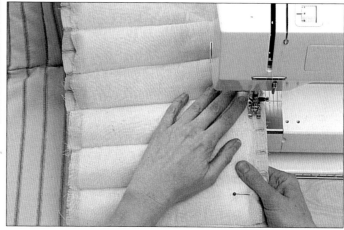

4 *With right sides together, stitch the cushion top to the strip, ¾ in (2 cm) from edge as shown, clipping into the strip at the corners (see p. 37). Attach bottom piece in the same way, leaving one end open to insert foam pad. Turn right sides out.*

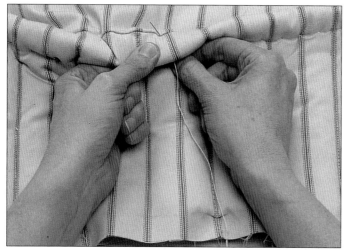

5 *Pin a 1¼-in (3-cm) pleat around top edge of cover and stitch it in place with stab stitches as shown every ½ in (1.5 cm) all around, pulling the two layers together very tightly.*

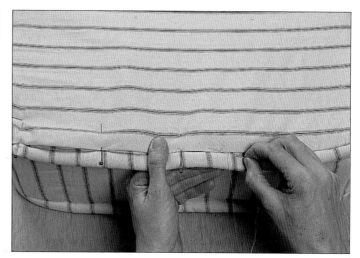

6 *Wrap the foam pad in batting (see p. 33) and secure batting to pad with big slipstitches (see p. 34). Insert pad, and stitch open end of cushion by hand as shown. Repeat Step 5 around bottom of cushion.*

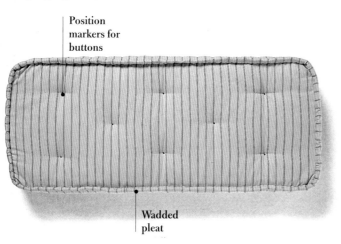

Position markers for buttons

Wadded pleat

7 *Using pins, mark positions for buttons on top and bottom of cushion. Use the cushion shape to design your pattern. Here we have mirrored the shape with six outside buttons and added two in the middle, making a criss-cross pattern.*

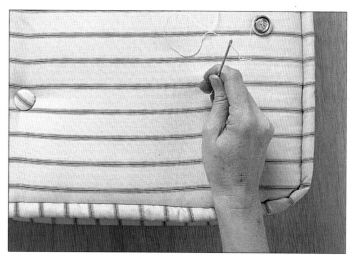

8 *Thread a mattress needle with strong button thread and tie a covered button (see p. 47) securely to one end.*

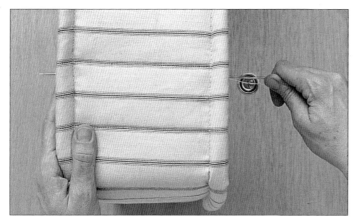

9 At the first marked button position, push the mattress needle through mattress, making sure that you keep it going straight so that it comes through the correct position on other side. Do not pull through.

10 Thread another button on other side of cushion as shown and push needle directly back through mattress. Pull thread tightly to embed both buttons in the cushion. Wind thread around button stand and use the needle to tie off tightly. Repeat at other marked button positions to finish. Spray with fabric protector before use.

BUTTON TUFT MATTRESS

As an alternative to buttons, you can make handmade tufts from wool or embroidery silk for a softer look. They are simple to make (see below) and are attached to the cushion in exactly the same way as the buttons (see Steps 8–10, p. 78 and above).

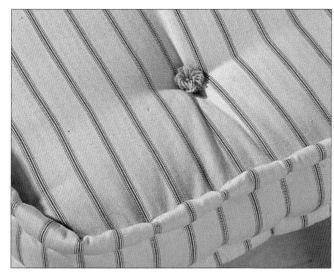

WHAT YOU WILL NEED

Follow list for Button Mattress on p. 77, replacing buttons with:

Wool or embroidery silk

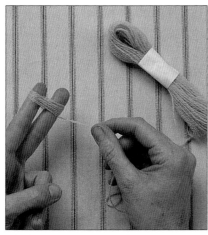

1 Hold two fingers ½ in (1.5 cm) apart and wind wool around tightly. The thickness of the wool governs how much you wind it around – wind fine wool 20 times, thick wool 10 times. Slide your fingers out of the skein.

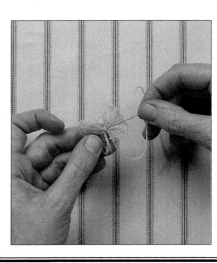

2 Wind wool around center of skein. Cut wool, thread needle onto end and make a few stitches in center to tie off. Attach as with buttons (see Steps 8–10, p. 78 and above).

LOOSE CHAIR COVER

A LOOSE CHAIR COVER is carefully tailored to fit snugly around the contours of a chair. Ties at the four corners of the seat keep the cover in place, while slits at the side are loose enough for the cover to be removed with ease when it needs to be washed.

You can use this cover on almost any type of upright chair to give it a new lease on life or to complement new furnishings or a color scheme. Alternatively, you could cover a number of nonmatching chairs in the same fabric to make them into a unique matching set for a dining-room table. For varied interest, you can cover the whole chair or, if there is a distinctive feature that you want to show off, such as the legs, you can adapt your pattern to leave them uncovered.

Strong weaves in relatively stiff, natural fibers, such as the cotton used here, help define a chair's geometric shape and are durable and easy to clean. For a luxurious feel you could use damask, adding a long gathered skirt to the hem and using satin ribbons for the ties.

WHAT YOU WILL NEED

Fabric

Chair cover
A piece cut to the size of the chair (see diagram for measuring chairs for loose covers on p. 28) plus ⅝ in (1.5 cm) around all edges

Accessories

Ties
Eight 1-in (2.5-cm) wide strips of cotton webbing to match cover fabric, each 14 in (35 cm) long

Making the cover

Cutting plan for chair cover (see also p. 28)

The positions of the ties (see Steps 6 and 7) are marked by *

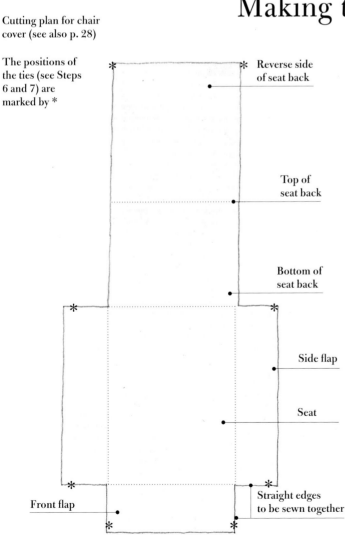

Reverse side of seat back

Top of seat back

Bottom of seat back

Side flap

Seat

Front flap

Straight edges to be sewn together

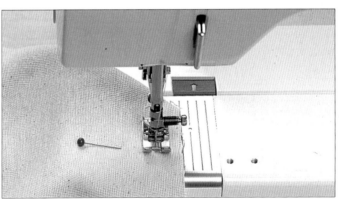

1 *To join front flap to side flaps at front of seat, lay the two straight edges right sides together. Pin and machine-stitch, taking a ⅝-in (1.5-cm) seam allowance and backstitching at each end to secure. Repeat for second flap.*

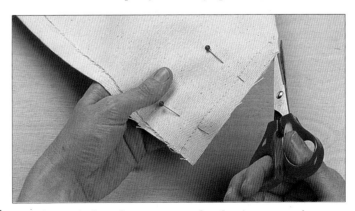

2 *Next, snip into the top corner of each miter, up to the seam line, as shown. Press open the seam.*

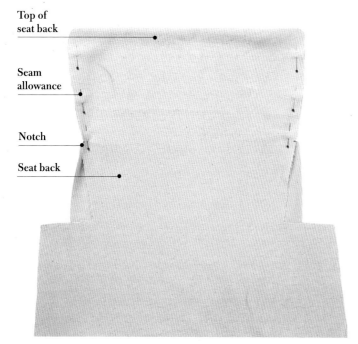

Top of
seat back

Seam
allowance

Notch

Seat back

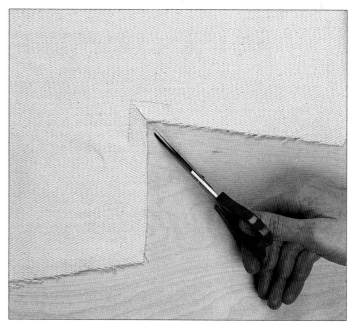

*3 Put cover on chair inside out and pin together the side
seams of the chair back as far down as possible, while still
allowing the cover to be removed easily. Snip a notch into seam
allowance where you will need to stop stitching. Remove cover
and machine-stitch side seams alongside pins from the top to
the notch. Stitch back and forth at notch to strengthen.*

*4 At back corners of the seat section, make a line of
reinforcing stitches around each corner, ⅝ in (1.5 cm)
in from the edge. Backstitch at each end. Snip diagonally
into each corner as shown.*

Machine-stitched
double hem

Machine-
stitched tie

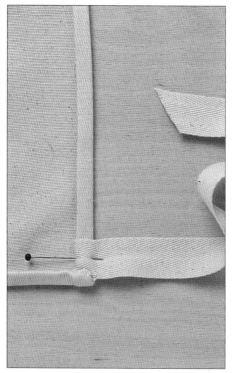

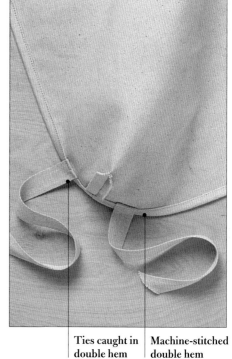

Ties caught in
double hem

Machine-stitched
double hem

*5 Pin a tie onto the two short edges of
the side flaps at the seat back, ⅝ in
(1.5 cm) from edge (see diagram on
p. 81). Press a double hem along raw
edges of inside corners up to seam on
chair back, first ¼ in (5 mm) then ⅜ in
(1 cm). Machine-stitch hem, making a
right-angled turn at corner. Use zigzag
stitch over raw edges (see inset).*

*6 Pin a tie at each bottom corner of the
cover back (see the diagram on
p. 81). Next, press and machine-stitch
a double hem down both side edges.
Repeat along bottom edge.*

*7 Pin remaining four ties for front
legs in position (see diagram on
p. 81), turn in a double hem all around
front edges, and machine-stitch,
catching all ties securely. To finish,
press and tie to chair.*

TWO-PIECE CHAIR COVER

As a pretty alternative to the all-in-one seat cover, here are separate covers for the seat and the back.
The seat cover stands alone as a quick removable cover to protect pristine upholstery or disguise
worn seats. The bottom edge of the back cover is scalloped to provide extra decorative detail.

WHAT YOU WILL NEED

Fabric

Cover for chair back
A piece cut to the size of the chair back, stopping 1 in
(2.5 cm) short of the seat (see diagram for measuring chairs for
loose covers on p. 28) plus ⅝ in (1.5 cm) around all edges

Facing for chair back
Two pieces cut to the width of the chair back x 6 in (15 cm)

Cover for chair seat
A piece cut to size of chair seat (including side, front, and back
flaps, see pp. 28, 81) plus ⅝ in (1.5 cm) around edges

Accessories

Ties
Eight 1-in (2.5-cm) wide strips of cotton webbing to
match cover fabric, each 14 in (35 cm) long

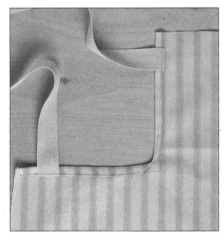

1 *Having joined the front corners of chair seat as in Steps 1–2 on p. 81, pin ties, press a double hem, and machine-stitch around edges as in Steps 4–7 on p. 82.*

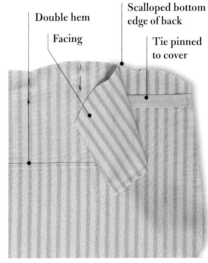

Double hem

Facing

Scalloped bottom edge of back

Tie pinned to cover

2 *Cut out scallop at bottom edges of back and facings. Stitch a double hem across straight edge of the facings and pin a tie to right sides of back in each bottom corner (4 ties in all). Pin facing sections to each end back with right sides together.*

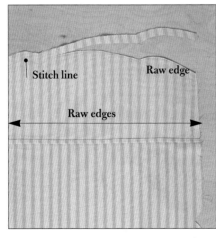

Stitch line

Raw edge

Raw edges

3 *Stitch around the three raw edges of each facing, taking a ⅝-in (1.5-cm) seam allowance. Backstitch at each end, ensuring you catch ties securely. Cut and clip seams around the curves.*

4 *With right sides together, fold the back in half, aligning bottom edges. Pin and stitch side seams to just above facings (see inset). Backstitch here to strengthen. Turn right side out, press curves, and attach to chair.*

BRAIDED SOFA DRAPE

THIS SOFA DRAPE is simple to make, using just two or three lengths of fabric joined with a French seam. It is designed to touch the floor on each side of the sofa. The hem is hidden behind a flat woven braid in a vividly contrasting color. This type of drape is useful when you want to cover up unattractive upholstery, herald a new season by changing the dark winter tones of your sofa to a lighter summer style, or simply protect it against the daily onslaught of children and pets. Perhaps you have just moved into a new home where your old sofa looks out of place, but your budget will not accommodate a replacement. Whatever your reasons, this throwover cover effects an instant transformation, and is surprisingly simple to make.

Consider a sturdy fabric that drapes over the back and arms. We have chosen a dramatic turquoise chenille because its texture and weight helps the throw to stay in position, and it is practically crease-proof. If you want to clean the cover regularly, use a washable, preshrunk fabric, with a washable, preshrunk, and colorfast braid.

The box pillows (see pp. 72–75 for instructions) sit separately on top of the throw. They help hold the throw in place and give the whole treatment a tailored and finished look.

WHAT YOU WILL NEED

Fabric

Measure the width of your sofa
(see p. 29 for measuring instructions)

Cut two lengths of fabric that together equal the sofa width, plus a 2-in (5-cm) seam allowance

If the width of fabric is less than half the depth of sofa (see p. 29), you will need 3 lengths of fabric

Accessories

Braid
Enough to go around the outside edge of the joined fabric

RAOUL DUFY - BAIE DES ANGES

Making the drape

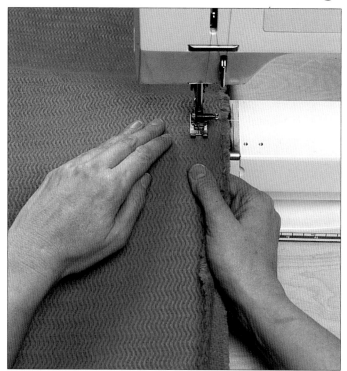

1 *Take the two lengths of fabric and stitch them together along one long side with right sides facing, taking a ⅝-in (1.5-cm) seam allowance. Stitch again to strengthen. Use a French seam (see p. 35) for heavy fabrics.*

2 *Arrange fabric over sofa. Make sure that seamline is in a position where it will be hidden by seat cushions, or tucked in at back of seat area. Mark a line where fabric breaks on the floor with pins. The fabric will need some careful arranging over the sofa arms but with some neat folding and pinning the bottom edge will look smart (see inset).*

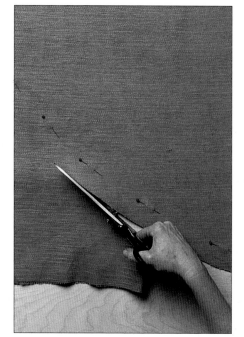

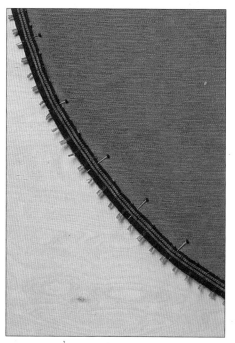

3 *Lay the fabric flat on a work surface and cut away excess fabric, leaving a 1-in (2.5-cm) seam allowance around pinned line.*

4 *Turn the work face down and press first a ¼-in (5-mm), then a ¾-in (2-cm) double hem. Machine-stitch.*

5 *Pin braid to the right side of fabric, around the hemmed edge. Machine-stitch in place along the top and bottom edges of the braid. To finish, press and arrange over sofa.*

SOFA DRAPE WITH TIES

*Ties embellish a sofa throw and hold the folds of fabric around
the arms of your sofa. Alternatively, use upholstery pins to hold the
throw in position and the ties for pure decoration.*

WHAT YOU WILL NEED

*Follow list for Braided Sofa Drape on p. 84.
In addition you will need:*

Braid

Enough to go around the outside edge of the
joined fabric, and an extra 4 strips of braid,
each 1 yd (90 cm) long

1 *Follow Steps 1–2, opposite. Then, while the throw
is still on the sofa, position the two braid ties on each
arm – here, the ties are aligned with the lower edge of the
sofa cushions. Pin them securely in place, tucking
under the ends.*

2 *Machine-stitch a square with a cross through it over
the tucked-under end of each tie to secure. Trim, hem,
and braid the bottom edge (see Steps 3–5 opposite). Press
and arrange over sofa to finish.*

PAISLEY WOOL THROW

U SING A THROW IS AN INGENIOUS way to add color, texture, and pattern to a room. You can spread it out flat across the back of a sofa, drape it over the arm of a chair, or display it neatly folded at the foot of a bed. Because you can move a throw from place to place, or even change it for another as the mood or season dictates, it offers you a unique freedom that is unlike other soft furnishings, curtains, or loose covers.

The wool fabric used here was chosen for its rich patterning. Because the throw is woven in a narrow width, the 3 in (7.5 cm) borders add much-needed breadth while allowing the reversible pattern to be visible on both sides.

Texture is of prime importance when choosing fabric for this style of throw. The fabric should drape and feel soft and inviting to the touch. Here we have bordered the fine and intricately woven reversible paisley wool with a contrasting fluid raw silk.

WHAT YOU WILL NEED

Fabric

Main piece
Finished width of throw minus 3 in (7.5 cm) x finished length of throw minus 3 in (7.5 cm)

Border
Joined 7-in (18-cm) wide bias-cut strips (see p. 40) the combined length of the finished throw's outside edges plus 24 in (60 cm)

Making the throw

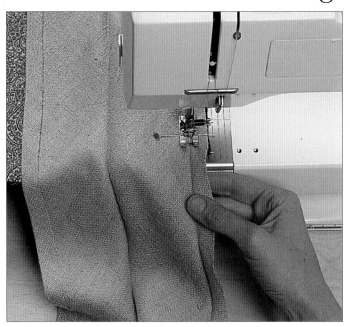

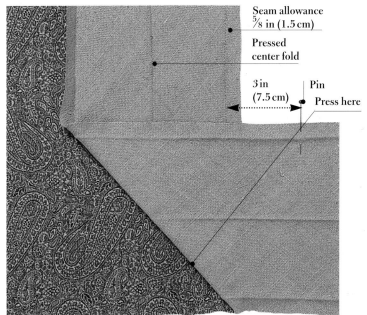

1 *Press a ⅝-in (1.5-cm) seam allowance along each side of border, then press it in half lengthwise with wrong sides facing. Open out and, with right sides together, pin border along one edge of main fabric, leaving at least 4 in (10 cm) extending beyond starting edge. Machine-stitch along fabric as shown, ⅝ in (1.5 cm) in from the edge and stopping ⅝ in (1.5 cm) short of the next side. Backstitch to secure, then remove from machine.*

2 *Next, create the miters (see pp. 38–39). Fold border diagonally away from main panel at a right angle and press lightly. Measure a distance equal to the width of the finished border – 3 in (7.5 cm) – from stitch line along the top edge of folded-over border, and mark that point with a pin.*

Seam allowance
⅝ in (1.5 cm)

Pressed center fold

3 in
(7.5 cm)

Pin
Press here

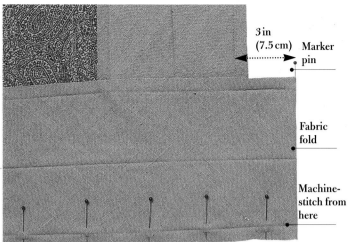

3 in (7.5 cm)

Marker pin

Fabric fold

Machine-stitch from here

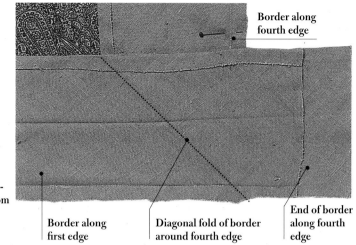

Border along fourth edge

Border along first edge

Diagonal fold of border around fourth edge

End of border along fourth edge

3 *Fold border to the left from marker pin, aligning edge of border with main fabric, forming a "T" shape. Pin and machine-stitch border from the fold along the side, backstitching to start, ⅝ in (1.5 cm) in from edge. Repeat Steps 2 and 3 around the third corner.*

4 *When you reach the fourth corner, diagonally fold the border fabric to form a right angle as at the other corners and then position it underneath the piece of border that you machine-stitched to the first edge of the main fabric in Step 1.*

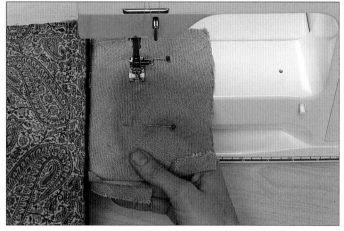

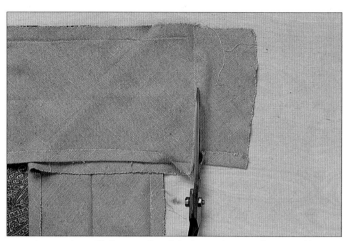

5 *Turn the work to the other side and pin together border ends. Machine-stitch together, 3 in (7.5 cm) away from the border stitch line.*

6 *Next, trim off the surplus fabric as close to the seamline as possible, taking care not to cut the stitching.*

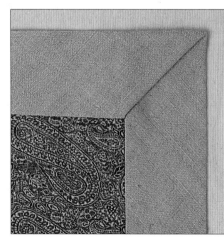

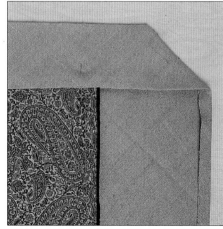

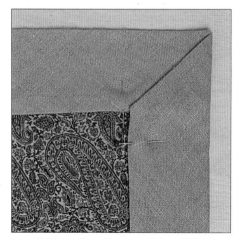

7 *Turn the work face up and fold the border over to the reverse side. The border will naturally form a miter at each corner. Lightly press each mitered corner.*

8 *Turn the border over to the other side of the throw and fold in the top and bottom of the border to meet the stitch line.*

9 *Fold in the other two sides of the border to complete the miters. Slipstitch (see p. 34) along inside edge of border and down each miter on both sides. Press to finish.*

TWO-TONED FRINGED THROW

*This throw is so uncomplicated that an absolute beginner could make it and achieve an
original and sophisticated result. Running stitch (see Step 3) prevents the two layers of fabric
from bagging out. Instead of the straight lines suggested here, you can follow the pattern
of the fabric or create your own pattern in running stitch.*

WHAT YOU WILL NEED

Fabric

Top layer
*Width of finished throw minus 2 in (5 cm) x length of
finished throw minus 2 in (5 cm)*

Bottom layer
Width of finished throw x length of finished throw

Accessories

Embroidery floss
Two stranded skeins

1 *First make a row of zigzag stitches
about ¾ in (2 cm) in from fabric
edge, all around the outside edge of
both pieces of fabric.*

2 *Fray raw edges of all sides of both
pieces of fabric, up to the zigzag
holding stitches. If your fabric doesn't
fray easily, snip into area being frayed
every 4 in (10 cm) or so, taking care
not to cut into zigzag stitches. This
gives you smaller areas to work on.*

3 *Lay the two layers of fabric flat,
wrong sides together. Stitch a row
of big running stitches (see p. 34)
around outside edge of throw to hold
layers together. Continue stitching
across center of fabric lengthwise, and
twice across width, dividing throw
into thirds. Press lightly to finish.*

CUBIC FOOTSTOOL

CHILDREN WILL LOVE this original addition to their playrooms. Made from a block of fire-resistant foam big enough to use as a stool but light enough for the youngest child to pick up and toss or roll around, this soft play cube will provide hours of energetic play while the appliquéd dice motif will encourage numeracy.

The cover needs to be made from a sturdy washable fabric that can withstand hard wear. We've used a strong sailcloth that was prewashed to prevent shrinkage at a later stage. This cube stands about 1 ft (30 cm) high, but if you want to create a larger cube you can simply increase the measurements and the circles accordingly. An alternative choice of fabric could be a wipe-clean vinyl on which you could forget the Velcro™ opening, and simply hand-sew the cover closed after inserting the foam.

WHAT YOU WILL NEED

Fabric

Main piece
$1\frac{1}{2}$ yd (1.5 m) of 48-in (1.2-m) wide fabric cut as in Step 1

Contrast fabric for spots
48 in (1.2 m) of 48-in (1.2-m) wide fabric cut as in Step 3

Accessories

Foam
14-in (36-cm) square block of fire-retardant foam

Bonding fabric
20 in (51 cm)

Velcro™
A strip 30 in (75 cm) long

Cup
$2\frac{1}{4}$–$2\frac{3}{4}$ in (6–7 cm) in diameter

Marker pen

Making the footstool

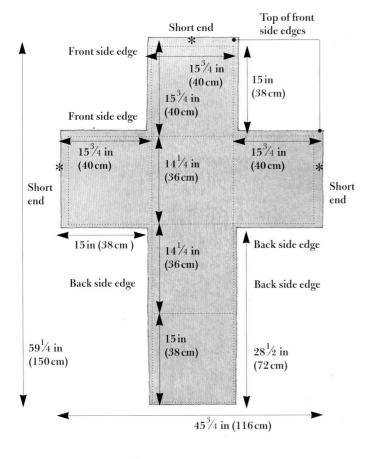

Short end
Top of front side edges

Front side edge
$15\frac{3}{4}$ in (40 cm)
15 in (38 cm)
$15\frac{3}{4}$ in (40 cm)

Front side edge

$15\frac{3}{4}$ in (40 cm)
$14\frac{1}{4}$ in (36 cm)
$15\frac{3}{4}$ in (40 cm)

Short end
Short end

15 in (38 cm)
$14\frac{1}{4}$ in (36 cm)
Back side edge

Back side edge
Back side edge

$59\frac{1}{4}$ in (150 cm)
15 in (38 cm)
$28\frac{1}{2}$ in (72 cm)

$45\frac{3}{4}$ in (116 cm)

All seam allowances are $\frac{3}{4}$ in (2 cm) except those at * which are $1\frac{1}{2}$ in (4 cm)

1 Using a ruler and tailor's chalk, mark and cut out the shape for the footstool cover using the dimensions shown above.

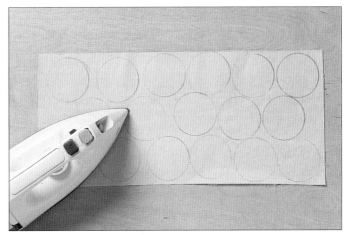

2 Place the bonding fabric on the wrong side of the contrast fabric. Using a cup and a marker pen, draw 21 circles.

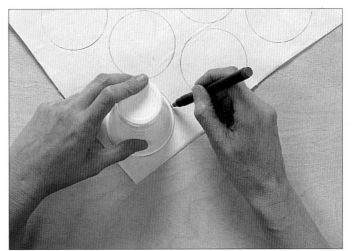

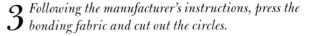

3 Following the manufacturer's instructions, press the bonding fabric and cut out the circles.

Use these circles as position guide for remaining sides

³/₄-in (2-cm) seam allowance

1 ½ in (4 cm) from fabric edge

4 *Use tailor's chalk to mark the position of the yellow circles, following the illustration. Begin by marking the six circles in the center so that the edge of the circles will be at least 1 ½ in (4 cm) in from fabric edge. Align the circles for the other sides with those marked for the six side.*

5 *Peel off the backing on the circles and lay them on the chalked marks on the main fabric, bonding fabric side down. Iron on. Satin-stitch around edge of each circle.*

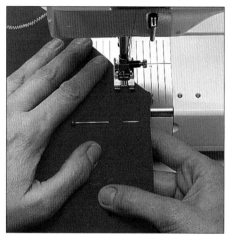

6 *Press a ½-in (1-cm) hem along three short ends of cross (see diagram on p. 93), right sides up. Pin and stitch the four side edges of cube right sides together, taking ³/₄-in (2-cm) seam allowances. Stop 1¼ in (3 cm) before pressed ends at top.*

7 *Snip into the diagonal fold in the seam at the four base corners of the cube (see diagram on p. 93) and press the seams open.*

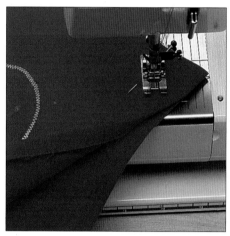

8 *At the top of the front side seams (see diagram on p. 93), stitch diagonally across the corner from where you stopped in Step 6 up to the top edge, going over the pressed hems. Backstitch several times to strengthen.*

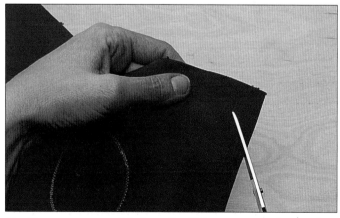

9 *To remove excess fabric, snip off the corners at the top of the front side seams (see diagram on p. 93). Snip close up to the diagonal stitching, but be careful not to cut into it. Press open the front side seams.*

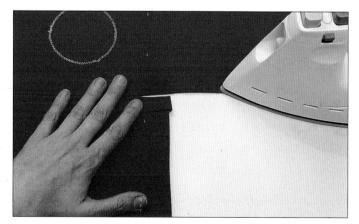

10 *On the two back side seams, backstitch several times at the top and press them open. Satin-stitch over the pressed seam to secure. Next, press a ³/₄-in (2-cm) hem to the wrong side around the three raw edges of the lid.*

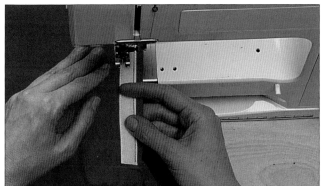

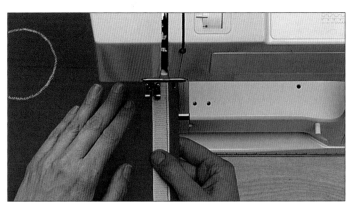

11 *Apply back of looped Velcro™ strips to wrong sides of lid (see diagram on p. 93), about ½ in (1 cm) in from folded edges. Machine-stitch Velcro™ edges so raw edges of hem are enclosed.*

12 *Apply hooked Velcro™ strips to right sides of fabric along top edges of cube, ½ in (1 cm) in from the folded edges, and machine-stitch so raw edges of hems are enclosed. Insert foam block and close Velcro™.*

ROPE-HANDLED PLAY CUBE

To help those little hands shift the play cube, we've added rope handles threaded through metal eyelets. Use contrasting rope handles as shown here, or choose a different color for each. The rope-handled cube adds a nautical touch to a room and helps you to combine it with other furnishings in traditional blue, yellow, and white.

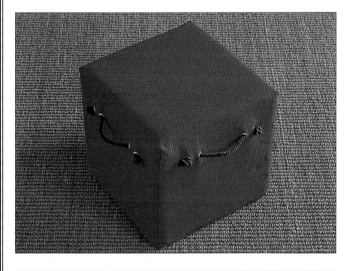

WHAT YOU WILL NEED

Fabric
1½ yd (1.5 m) of 48-in (1.2-m) wide fabric, cut as in Step 1, p. 93

Accessories

Foam
14-in (36-cm) square block of fire-retardant foam

Velcro™
A strip 30 in (75 cm) long

Eyelets
Sixteen, ½ in (1 cm) in diameter

Rope
1½ yd (1.5 m)

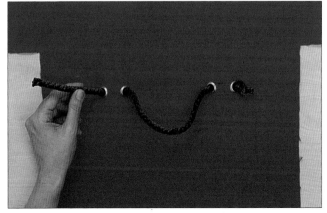

1 *Mark eyelet positions in chalk on each side of cover, 3 in (7.5 cm) down from foldline that will form top edge of cube, and cut out. The two inner marks are 5 in (12.5 cm) apart, and the outer two 1½ in (4 cm) away from those. Follow manufacturer's instructions for hammering in eyelets.*

2 *Cut the rope into four equal lengths. Knot one end and thread through the eyelets before knotting the other end. Repeat on all four sides. To finish, follow main project from Step 6.*

Throwover Bedspread

The simplest kind of bedspread consists of a flat expanse of fabric that drapes over the bed and drops down the sides and end of the bed, reaching almost to the floor. The corners of the spread at the foot of the bed are cut in a curve so that they just skim the floor. We've added a deep natural-linen fringe around the hem.

This bedspread is ideal for a divan, or a bed without a footboard. If your bed has a decorative headboard or frame, the bedspread can be tucked in under the mattress all the way around. But if you have a pretty bed skirt that you would like to show, you can make your bedspread extend only halfway to the floor. In both these instances, the essential shape of the bedspread is rectangular and you can omit the instructions for curving the corners.

It is best to use a fabric that has weight and does not crease too badly, but you can counteract these effects by lining or even quilting the spread. This also makes your spread reversible and is particularly helpful if you need to protect the back of a bedspread constructed from patchwork or a loose-weave fabric.

The calming influence of a harmonious color scheme suits a bedroom, so it is useful to coordinate the bedspread with curtains and other furnishings.

WHAT YOU WILL NEED

Fabric

Main pieces

*Two pieces the length of the bed plus depth to floor
(see p.30) plus 3 in (7.5 cm), less the fringe depth*

Allow extra fabric if there is a pattern to match

Accessories

Fringe

Enough to go around three edges of the main fabric

Pencil

String

The depth to floor plus 6 in (15 cm)

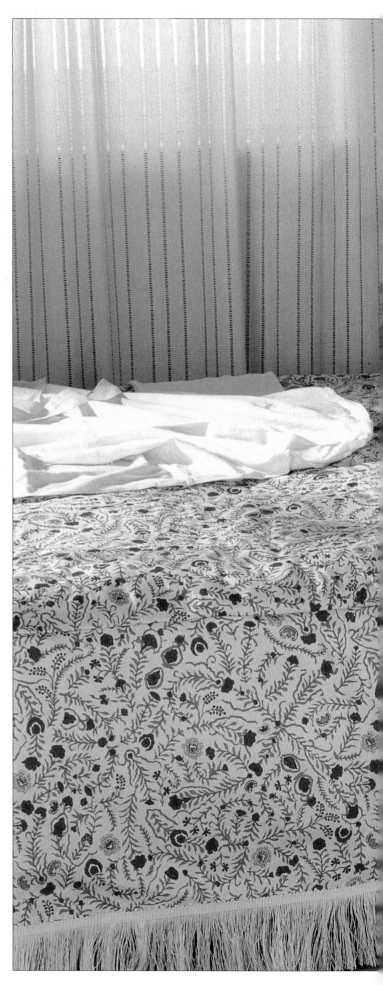

Making the bedspread

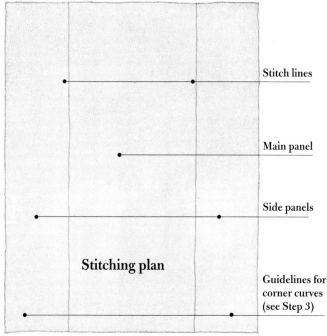

Stitch lines

Main panel

Side panels

Stitching plan

Guidelines for corner curves (see Step 3)

This diagram shows how the fabric is cut and stitched to form the bedspread.

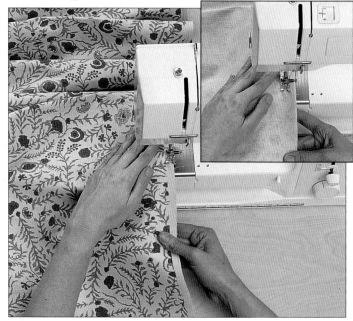

1 *Form the two side panels of the bedspread by cutting one of the lengths of fabric down the center lengthwise. The other length of fabric forms the main panel.*

2 *Next, make the French seams (see p. 35). With wrong sides together, machine-stitch the side panels to the main panel, matching any pattern. Trim seam allowances to ¼ in (5 mm) and press open. Fold at seamlines, right sides together, and machine-stitch ½ in (1 cm) in from the fold (see inset).*

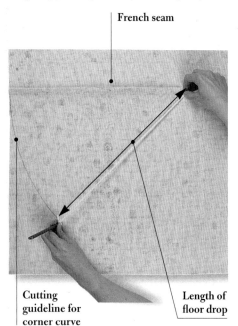

French seam

Cutting guideline for corner curve

Length of floor drop

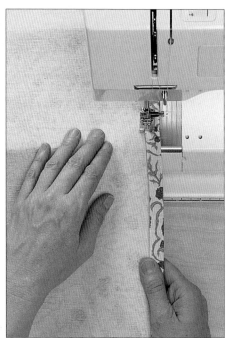

3 *To trim the front and sides of the spread, center it on the bed. Allowing for a 1-in (2.5-cm) seam allowance and the fringe drop, pin the fabric to mark cutting line and cut on all three sides. Fold the spread in half lengthwise, right sides together, and mark the corner curves using a pencil and string as shown (see also p.32). Cut along pencil line.*

4 *Make a ½-in (1-cm) double hem around sides and end of spread, machine-stitching close to inner folded edge on wrong side. Make a 1-in (2.5-cm) double hem across pillow end of the spread and machine-stitch in the same way.*

5 *Attach the fringing by hand around the sides and end. To finish, fold under raw edges of fringe twice and slipstitch (see p.34) in place to prevent unravelling. Press the bedspread before use.*

BEDSPREAD WITH COVERED SEAMS

This bedspread is made with fabric cut in the same way as the cover opposite, but using a standard ⅝-in (1.5-cm) seam allowance. A standard seam, made on the right side of the cover, is hidden by bias-cut contrast fabric, which is also used as a decorative binding on the hem. The corners at the foot of the bed are rounded as described in Step 3, opposite.

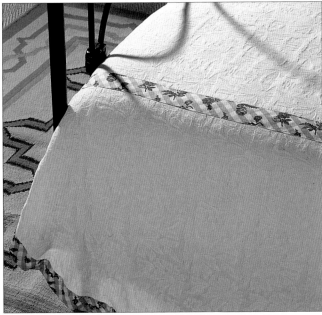

WHAT YOU WILL NEED

Fabric

Main piece
Follow the instructions on p. 96, but do not subtract the fringe depth

Contrast Fabric
Joined bias-cut strips, 3 in (7.5 cm) wide (see p. 40) to go around three sides of the bedspread and two to go along the length of the bedspread

Accessories
Pencil

String
The depth to floor plus 6 in (15 cm)

1 *Follow Step 1, p.98 to join main fabric, leaving a ⅝-in (1.5-cm) seam allowance. Fold a ½-in (1-cm) seam along each long edge of joined bias-cut strips. Pin over seams and baste as shown, then machine-stitch edges of each strip.*

2 *Curve bottom corners as in Step 3, opposite. With wrong sides together and a ½-in (1-cm) seam allowance, stitch the rest of bias strip to edge of spread. Start at one top corner and work around to other top corner. Press seam open.*

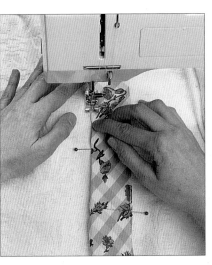

3 *Press open the ½-in (1-cm) seam along other edge of border as shown. Fold the border edge over sewn seam to meet vertical bias strip.*

4 *Pin and baste in place, working around the edge. Finally machine-stitch close to border and main fabric join (see inset). Press on reverse side of fabric before use.*

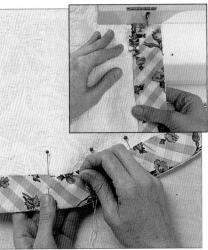

GATHERED BED VALANCE

A BED VALANCE GIVES an impression of generosity, carrying the texture and often the pattern of the bedcover fabric right through to the floor. A valance is made to fit the base of a bed, concealing the base and anything kept underneath it. The gathered skirt is attached to an inexpensive fabric, such as calico or lining fabric, and runs around three sides of the bed and 1 cm (6 in) into each corner at the head of the bed.

If your bed has a footboard but you wish to conceal the sides of the bed, you can adapt the project to omit the instructions for the skirt section at the end of the bed.

Valances can be used to match or contrast the fabric of the bedcover and in particular the floor covering. For best results, choose a fabric that supports and accentuates the gathers. However, try to avoid thick, stiff fabrics that are difficult to manipulate. If you decide upon a lightweight fabric to coordinate with your decor, you can line the skirt for extra body.

WHAT YOU WILL NEED

Fabric

Skirt
Widths of fabric joined with French seams (see p.35) the distance round the bed plus head end (see diagram below and p. 30), multiplied by two times the depth to the floor, plus 6.5 cm (2 ½ in)

Border panel
Two 18-cm (7-in) deep joined widths of fabric, each the length of the bed; two 18-cm (7-in) deep pieces of fabric, each 15 cm (6 in) long; one 18-cm (7-in) deep piece of fabric the width of the bed

Top panel
Same dimensions as the top of the bed base plus 1.5 cm (⅝ in) all around, in lining fabric

Accessories
Small cup
Pencil

Making the valance

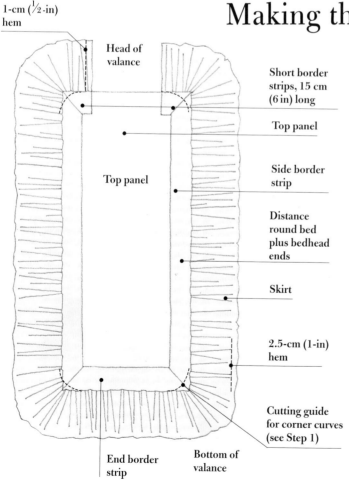

1-cm (½-in) hem

Head of valance

Short border strips, 15 cm (6 in) long

Top panel

Side border strip

Top panel

Distance round bed plus bedhead ends

Skirt

2.5-cm (1-in) hem

Cutting guide for corner curves (see Step 1)

End border strip

Bottom of valance

This diagram shows how the valance looks when it is complete. Refer to it when doing Steps 1 and 6–12

1 *Use a small cup to draw a curve at the corners of the top panel as shown. Using scissors, cut round the pencil line.*

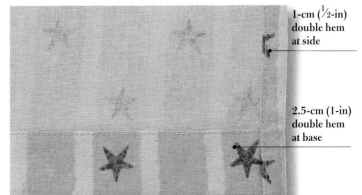

1-cm (½-in) double hem at side

2.5-cm (1-in) double hem at base

2 *On the skirt, press and machine stitch a 2.5-cm (1-in) double hem on the bottom and a double 1-cm (½-in) hem at each side.*

Notch snipped in
seam allowance

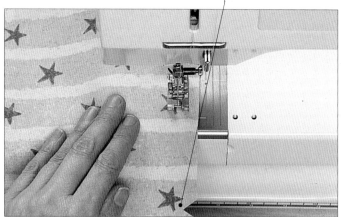

3 *Snip notches in the seam allowance of raw edge of skirt at 24-in (60-cm) intervals (see diagram, right). Gather stitch ½ in (1 cm) in from raw edge. Begin and end at each snip.*

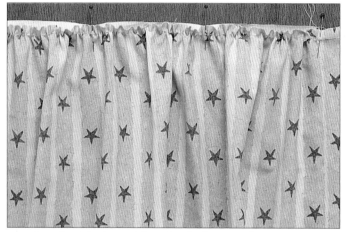

4 *Starting 6 in (15 cm) in at head of top panel, snip into seam allowance at 12-in (30-cm) intervals. Match notches on both fabrics and pin, wrong sides together. Pull gathering stitches between each snip (see p. 43).*

This diagram shows how you attach the bed skirt to the top panel.

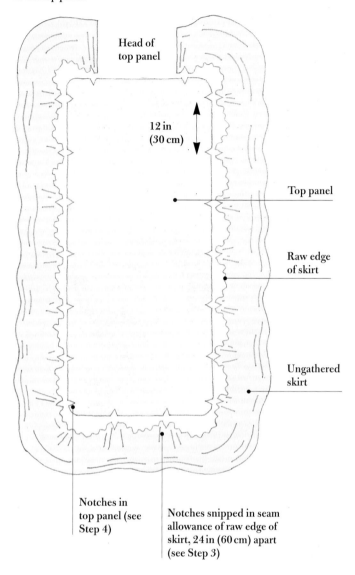

Head of
top panel

12 in
(30 cm)

Top panel

Raw edge
of skirt

Ungathered
skirt

Notches in
top panel (see
Step 4)

Notches snipped in seam
allowance of raw edge of
skirt, 24 in (60 cm) apart
(see Step 3)

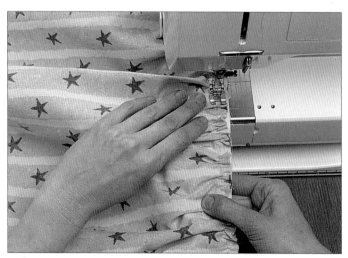

5 *Make sure that the gathers are evenly spaced and machine-stitch the skirt to the top panel.*

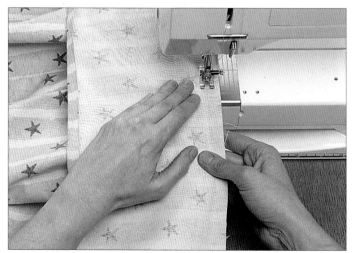

6 *Press a ⅝-in (1.5-cm) hem down one long side of each border strip and, with right sides together and a ⅝-in (1.5-cm) seam allowance, stitch end border strip to bottom of bed skirt (see diagram, p. 101). Stop midway at curved corners; attach side borders to each side and the short borders at the head.*

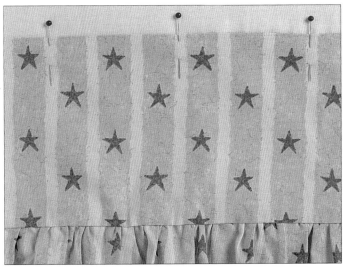

7 *Place the bed skirt right side up on a flat surface. Fold over border strips to top panel and pin the pressed edge of border to the top as shown.*

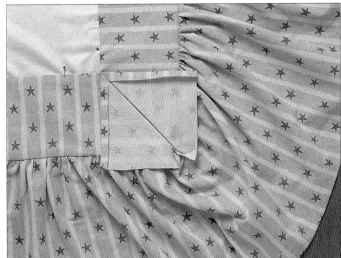

8 *To miter the corners, fold out the excess fabric to form a diagonal seam. Press the seam open.*

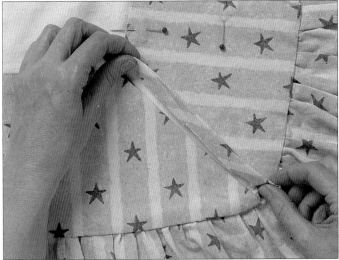

9 *Trim away excess fabric and turn under raw edges ⅝ in (1.5 cm).*

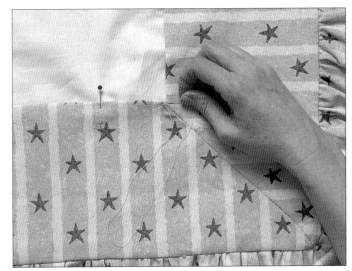

10 *Slipstitch (see p. 34) the diagonal seam by hand as shown, keeping the fabric flat as you work.*

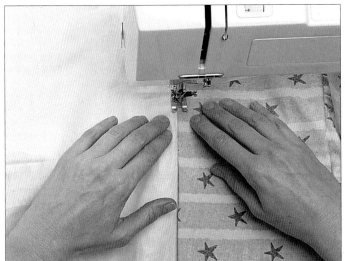

11 *Next, machine-stitch the inside edge of the border strips to the top panel as shown.*

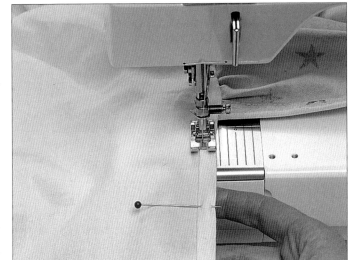

12 *On wrong side of fabric, pin and stitch a ⅝-in (1.5-cm) double hem along raw edge of top panel between the two ends of the skirt. Fit onto bed.*

HEADBOARD
COVER

T HIS WHITE LINEN COVER would add a touch of simple elegance to any bedroom. It hangs over the top of the headboard and is held in place with pretty decorative ties down each side.

The cover is designed for a rectangular padded headboard with no shaping along the top. The sides of the headboard are exposed, so if you are using an existing headboard you may want to re-cover it with a plain calico or ticking. This is not a difficult task, but you will need a heavy-duty staple gun. Alternatively, have a padded headboard made to measure by an upholstery firm, and ask them to cover it in calico.

Although a crisp white linen is used here, white need not be an impractical choice — any washable fabric is suitable since this cover is easily removable for regular washing along with other bed linen. As an alternative, and to further emphasize the facing detail, you can cut the facings and ties in a contrasting fabric that picks up colors or patterns used elsewhere in the room.

WHAT YOU WILL NEED

Fabric

Cover depth
Twice the distance between the top of the mattress and the top of the headboard, plus the thickness of the headboard, plus 1 ½ in (4 cm)

Cover width
The width of the headboard plus 1 ¼ in (3 cm) – if your fabric is narrower than the headboard width, sew two lengths of fabric together (see Steps 1–2, p. 98)

Facing strips
Two 3-in (8-cm) strips the depth of the cover

Ties
Twelve 1 ¼-in (3-cm) wide bias-cut strips (see p. 40), each 14 in (35 cm) long

Accessories

Rouleau turner or safety pin

Making the cover

Tie folded in half and stitched

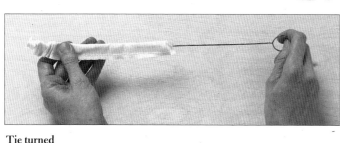

Tie turned right side out and knotted

1 *Make the twelve ties by folding each strip in half lengthwise with right sides together. Stitch ¼ in (5 mm) from raw edges. Turn right side out using a rouleau turner (see p. 41) or safety pin. Tuck in the raw edges at one end and tie a knot to finish.*

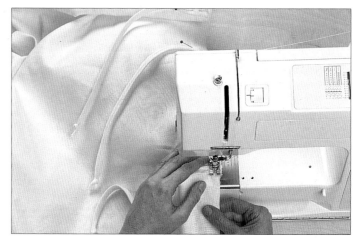

2 *Place cover fabric over headboard and mark with a pin where each pair of ties will be stitched. Remove cover, check evenness of spacing, and pin unfinished end of each tie on right side of cover fabric, aligning raw edges. Make a few backstitches over end of each tie, keeping within ⅝-in (1.5-cm) seam allowance.*

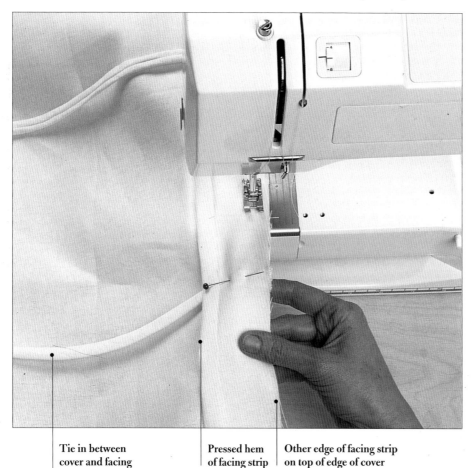

Tie in between cover and facing strip

Pressed hem of facing strip

Other edge of facing strip on top of edge of cover

3 *Taking one of the facing strips, press over a ⅝-in (1.5-cm) hem along one of the long raw edges. Then pin the other edge of the facing strip to one side of the cover, right sides together. Stitch together with a ⅝-in (1.5-cm) seam allowance, machine-stitching over the ends of the ties.*

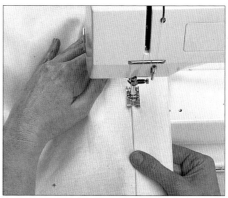

4 *Turn the facing over to the wrong side of the cover fabric and press. Topstitch close to the outside edge of the facing and then close to the inside folded edge. Repeat Steps 3–4 for the other side of the cover.*

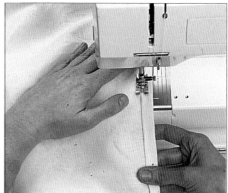

5 *For the hems of the cover, press a ½-in (1-cm) double hem to the wrong side at both ends and machine-stitch. Press to finish and place over headboard.*

PADDED HEADBOARD COVER

This padded headboard cover is perfect for transforming a hard wooden headboard, or even a metal bedstead. The large pad has a removable loose cover and includes ties to secure it at each side.

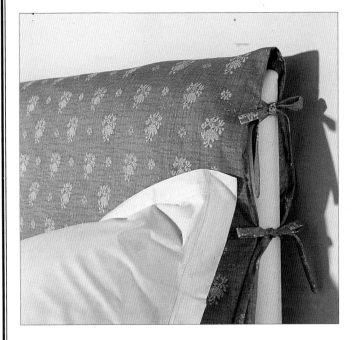

WHAT YOU WILL NEED

Fabric

Main fabric length
Twice the distance between the top of the mattress and top of the headboard, plus the thickness of the headboard, plus 12 ½ in (32 cm)

Main fabric width
As for main project (see p. 104)

Lining fabric
As for main fabric (see p. 104)

Ties
As for main project (see p. 104)

Accessories

Rouleau turner or safety pin

Polyester filling
1 ¾ lb (800g)

Snap-fastener tape
The width of the headboard

1 *Fold lining fabric in half widthwise and sew down each side and partly across bottom, leaving a 12-in (30-cm) opening. Turn right side out and stuff with polyester filling. Machine-stitch over opening to close (see inset).*

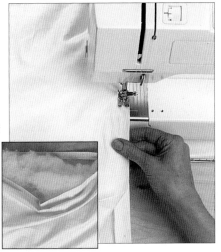

2 *Make sure that filling is evenly distributed. Hand-sew long running stitches with strong button thread (see inset). Sew down the pad, dividing it into three equal sections. Make the ties as in Step 1, p. 106.*

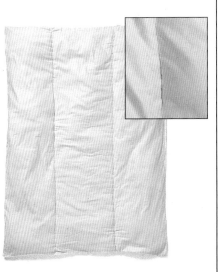

3 *Place cover over headboard, then mark positions of ties and stitch as shown (see Step 2, p. 106). Machine-stitch each side of the cover, and press a hem ⅝ in (1.5 cm) along opening at the bottom.*

4 *Pin and stitch one side of snap-fastener tape along one side of the opening. Repeat on other side to finish, ensuring the snaps match. Insert pad.*

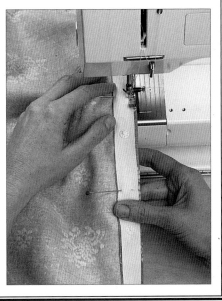

SINGLE QUILT COVER

HERE IS A TRADITIONAL brushed cotton quilt cover made to a pieced design, reminiscent of early American patchworks. The buttoned opening for the cover lies across the front of the quilt near the top, and contrasting colored buttons give added emphasis.

Ready-made quilt covers are available in an exciting range of colors and designs, but it can be difficult to re-create the effect when sewing at home. In addition to the problem of finding fabric wide enough, the amount of fabric needed can make this undertaking impractical. However, a pieced design or patchwork allows you to use fabric economically, especially if you are using leftover fabric from other projects.

Patchwork can be intricate, but we have taken a shortcut by using large pieces in different but coordinating checks of brushed cotton shirting. The underside of a quilt cover should be smooth against the skin, so if you are short of main fabric you could use a sheet. The overriding consideration when choosing fabrics is that they should be preshrunk and colorfast.

Here, the checks give an illusion of more detailed patchwork while the brushed cotton is a cozy choice of fabric for bedding.

WHAT YOU WILL NEED

Finished quilt size 55 in (140 cm) wide x 78 in (200 cm) long

Fabric

Fabric A
1 square 19 x 19 in
(49 x 49 cm)
4 triangles $35\frac{3}{4}$ x $25\frac{3}{8}$ x $25\frac{3}{8}$ in
(91 x 64.5 x 64.5 cm)
3 rectangles 9 x $11\frac{1}{4}$ in
(23 x 28 cm)

Fabric B
4 triangles $20\frac{1}{4}$ x $14\frac{1}{2}$ x
$14\frac{1}{2}$ in (51 x 36.5 x 36.5 cm)
4 squares $5\frac{1}{4}$ x $5\frac{1}{4}$ in
(13 x 13 cm)
4 strips $48\frac{1}{4}$ x $5\frac{1}{4}$ in
(123 x 13 cm)
2 button plackets $56\frac{1}{4}$ x $5\frac{1}{4}$ in
(143 x 13 cm), cut on the bias

Fabric C
4 strips $26\frac{1}{2}$ x $5\frac{1}{4}$ in
(68 x 13 cm)
4 squares $5\frac{1}{4}$ x $5\frac{1}{4}$ in (13 x 13 cm)
4 rectangles 9 x $11\frac{1}{4}$ in
(23 x 28 cm)

Underside piece
1 piece $56\frac{1}{4}$ x $90\frac{1}{4}$ in
(143 x 233 cm)

Accessories
Iron-on interfacing
$1\frac{1}{2}$ yd (1.5 m)

Buttons
Six

Making the quilt cover

Quilt design

■ Fabric A   ▦ Fabric B

■ Fabric C

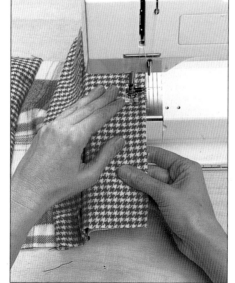

1 *Using the diagram as a guide, with right sides together and always taking a ⅝-in (1.5-cm) seam allowance, machine-stitch the pieces of the patchwork together (see also Step 2).*

2 *As you complete each seam, press the seam allowances outward, turn the work to the right side, and topstitch close to the seam through all layers as shown. This reinforces each seam.*

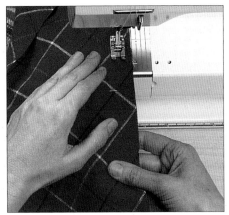

3 *With right sides together, machine-stitch one of the bias-cut button placket pieces along the top edge of the patchwork.*

4 *Press the seam allowances toward the placket. Turn the work over to the right side and topstitch close to the seam as shown.*

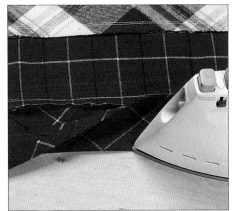

5 *Turn the work back to the wrong side and press over a ⅝-in (1.5-cm) hem along the long raw edge of placket piece. Then press the whole placket in half so that the folded edge meets the seamline.*

6 *Slipstitch (see p. 34) the placket by hand to the main fabric. Set this fabric piece aside.*

7 *Iron on a strip of lightweight interfacing to wrong side of the other placket piece, being careful not to stretch the bias. This is to add reinforcement for the buttonholes.*

8 *With right sides together and taking a ⅝-in (1.5-cm) seam allowance, stitch the interfaced placket to one end of the underside piece and continue as in Steps 4, 5, and 6 to finish the placket.*

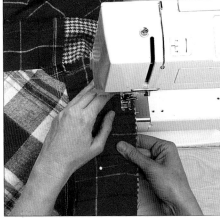

9 *With underside piece right side up, fold 14 in (35 cm) (including the placket) over at top and lay patchwork piece face down on top of it, aligning bottom edges and sides. The placket pieces should overlap. Pin and machine-stitch together side and bottom seams.*

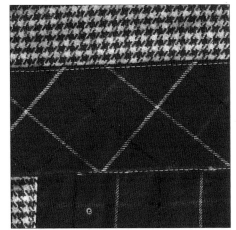

10 *Turn right side out and mark and sew the six button and buttonholes on plackets, spacing them evenly and following the instructions on page 47. Press on reverse to finish.*

PATCHWORK QUILT

This snugly padded, tufted quilt is made to the same patchwork design as the
main project (see p. 109). The lighter check on the underside emphasizes the quilted look.

WHAT YOU WILL NEED

Finished quilt size 55 in (140 cm) wide
x 65 in (165 cm) long

Fabric
(see diagram on p.109)

Fabric A
As for main project (see p.109)

Fabric B
As for main project (see p.109)
but with no plackets

Fabric C
As for main project plus
6 ¾ yd (6 m) of 2-in (5-cm)
wide joined bias-cut strips

Underside piece
One piece of fabric measuring
56 ¼ x 66 ¼ in
(143 x 168 cm)

Accessories
Piping cord
7 yd (6.5 m)

Tapestry wool
Two skeins
in contrasting colors

Spray adhesive

Batting
Enough to fit finished
quilt size

1 *Make the patch-*
work (see Step 1,
p. 109), pressing
each seam open as
you go and attach
piping around the
edge (see p. 52) on
the right side. With
the patchwork face
down, apply spray
adhesive over it and
stick down a layer
of batting.

2 *Lay patch-*
work face up,
and place the
underside piece
face down on top.
Pin and machine-
stitch around the
edges using a
zipper foot. Leave
an opening at one
end. Turn right
side out and
hand-stitch
the opening.

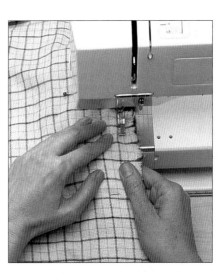

3 *Lay quilt*
right side up.
Mark position of
tufts with pins – at
the corners of the
inner and outer
squares. Thread a
tapestry needle and,
stitching with four
strands at a time,
take a stitch through
all layers of the
quilt. Tie wool into
a double knot.

4 *Trim the*
strands of wool
1 in (2.5 cm) above
the knot. Fan the
strands out.
Continue making
the remaining 7
tufts to finish.

TABLECLOTH WITH A BORDER

HERE IS A PRETTY idea for making a tablecloth for a dining table. A cream cotton damask is edged with a silk border carefully cut into scallop shapes and mitered at each corner.

The choice of gold dupion silk for the border gives this tablecloth its grand style. For day-to-day use, choose a less glamorous border fabric, such as a narrow cream stripe. The border needs to be made from a lightweight fabric that will mold easily into the scallop shapes. Because this tablecloth is delicately constructed, it should only be hand-washed. Make sure that the fabrics you choose have been preshrunk and are colorfast (see p. 124). Wash the fabrics again before making your tablecloth, just to be sure that they do not shrink – even minimal shrinkage can cause puckering. This is important, as the scallops need to drape delicately over your table.

This tablecloth is designed for a rectangular dining table. To adapt the idea for a round or oval table, cut the border on the bias so that you can ease it around the curve.

WHAT YOU WILL NEED

Fabric

Main piece

The width of the table plus 13¼ in (33 cm) x the length of the table plus 13¼ in (33 cm)

To ensure a perfect fit, make the border first and then cut out the main piece to fit exactly with a ⅝-in (1.5-cm) overlap around each edge

Border pieces

Four 7-in (17.5-cm) wide strips the width of the table plus 14 in (35 cm) and four 7-in (17.5-cm) wide strips the length of the table plus 14 in (35 cm)

Accessories

Pencil

Small bowl or plate
Approximate diameter of 5½ in (13.5 cm)

Book or piece of paper

Making the tablecloth

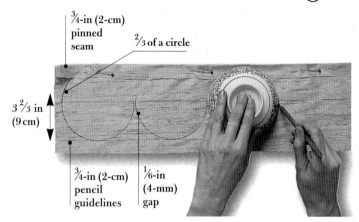

¾-in (2-cm) pinned seam

⅔ of a circle

3⅔ in (9 cm)

¾-in (2-cm) pencil guidelines

⅙-in (4-mm) gap

1 *With fabric right side down, press a ¾-in (2-cm) seam along one long edge of all border strips. Pin two strips right sides together. Draw two pencil guidelines as shown, then draw around bowl to make a row of semicircles, leaving ⅙ in (4 mm) between each. Start and finish with two-thirds of a circle.*

2 *Set the machine to a small stitch length and sew around scallops, blunting the point where they meet by making a few horizontal stitches. Carefully trim fabric around scallops, leaving a ⅙-in (4-mm) seam allowance. Snip close, but take care not to cut any stitches.*

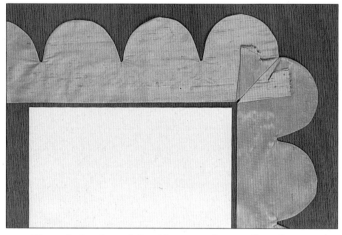

3 *Turn the borders right side out and press. Lay them on a flat surface at right angles, using a book or piece of paper as a guide. Fold out the fabric edges to 45° and press to form a diagonal seam.*

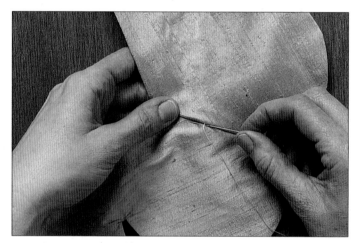

4 *Trim excess fabric, turn under raw edges, and slipstitch the diagonal seam together on one side of the fabric. Turn the work over and slipstitch the other side.*

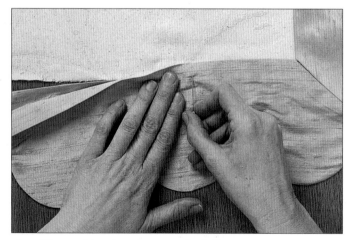

5 *After making four corners, check the measurements between each inside corner. Cut main fabric to these measurements plus ⅝-in (1.5-cm) seam allowance on all sides. Insert, pin, and baste main fabric between the two layers of border.*

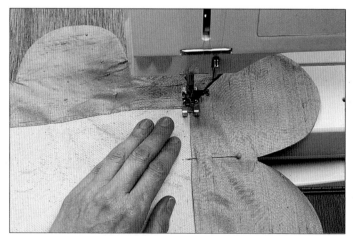

6 *Machine-stitch all sides through all layers close to the inside edge of the border. Make sure that your stitches catch the reverse side of the border. Press on reverse to finish.*

TABLECLOTH WITH A ZIGZAG BORDER

This zigzag border cloth can be made with primary-colored fabrics for a children's birthday party or even a medieval banquet. Alternatively, choose subtle pastels for a classic contrast to the bold design.

WHAT YOU WILL NEED

Fabric
Follow list for Tablecloth with a Border (see p.112) for fabric measurements

Accessories
Tailor's chalk

Ruler

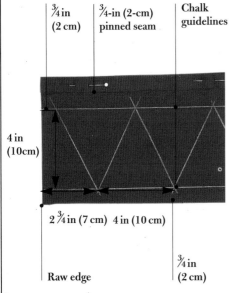

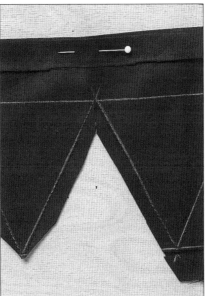

1 *Prepare the border strips as in Step 1, p. 114. Draw two chalk guidelines, then mark and draw in the position of the zigzags, using the measurements shown above.*

2 *Machine-stitch along the zigzag chalk line, blunting the corners by stitching one stitch square across the point. Trim away excess fabric, snipping close in to each point. Take care not to cut any stitches.*

3 *Turn the borders right side out and lay out on a flat surface. Follow Steps 3 and 4 for the scalloped border on p. 114, then Steps 5 and 6 to form the mitered corners by hand and to insert the main fabric of the tablecloth. Press on reverse to finish.*

CIRCULAR TABLECLOTH WITH SQUARE TOP CLOTH

A FULL-LENGTH CIRCULAR TABLECLOTH covering an occasional table provides an excellent setting for family photographs and special ornaments. This design can also be scaled down for a bedroom side table displaying clocks, lamps, or books. As the table is entirely hidden by the long tablecloth, you can disguise the roughest particle board to create a beautiful yet cost-effective item.

The full-length circular cloth has a top cloth that is square and edged with a 1-in (2.5-cm) wide contrasting border. Each corner of the top cloth is trimmed with a tassel, and the hanging loop of each is stitched into a heart motif.

The tablecloth needs to brush the floor, so take extra care with your measurements and do not underestimate — it is better to add an additional ½ in (1 cm) than to let the tablecloth swing above the floor.

For the top cloth use a washable fabric, as it is traditionally the protective covering for the more elaborate tablecloth. Remove the heart tassels before washing. Here, the tablecloth is made from a subtle cotton print that coordinates with the bold, directional effect of the striped top cloth.

WHAT YOU WILL NEED

Fabric

Main fabric for top cloth
Diameter of table plus 10 in (25 cm) square

Border for top cloth
4-in (10-cm) wide joined bias-cut strips (see p. 40) the combined length of the edges of the top cloth plus 2 in (5 cm)

Tablecloth
Diameter of table plus twice the distance from tabletop to floor, plus 1 in (2.5 cm) for hems square

If you need to join two fabric lengths (see p. 98), allow 1 in (2.5 cm) extra for hems

Accessories

Tassels
Four

Pencil

String

Making the tablecloth

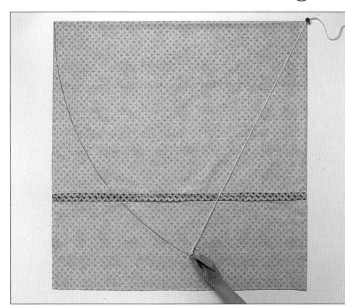

1 *Take the fabric for the tablecloth and fold it in half length-wise and again widthwise. Draw a quarter circle along unfolded edge as shown, using pencil and string (see p. 32).*

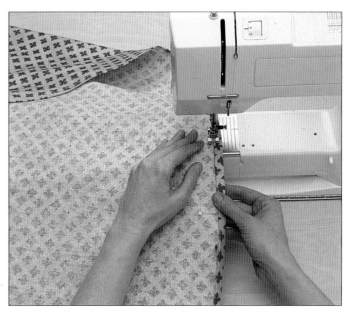

2 *Cut along the pencil line and open out the fabric into a full circle. Press a ½-in (1-cm) double hem around edge of tablecloth and machine-stitch.*

Making the top cloth

1 Press the border strip in half lengthwise and open out. Press in raw edges to meet center fold as shown and open out again.

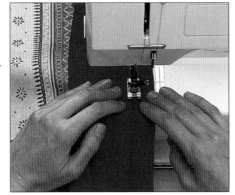

2 Place border down one side of main fabric, right sides together, aligning raw edges. Stitch 1 in (2.5 cm) from start along first foldline (made in Step 1), stopping 1 in (2.5 cm) before corner and backstitching.

3 Diagonally fold border away from main fabric at a right angle and press lightly.

4 Fold border back over so that it aligns with next edge of main fabric. Pin in position and stitch from fold along outside foldline. Repeat process along other edges.

5 Stitch up to 4 in (10 cm) from final corner. Fold starting border piece as in Step 3 and overlay final border piece. Pin as shown.

6 Turn fabric to reverse side and machine-stitch. Trim seam to ⅝ in (1.5 cm) (see inset).

7 Fold over border along central fold line onto other side of main fabric, forming a neat miter at each corner on the front of the throw as shown. Press lightly, pin, and slipstitch miter (see p. 39).

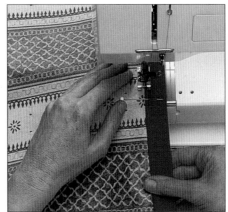

8 On the right side of the fabric, machine-stitch close to inside edge of border, making sure that the fabric at the back is being stitched at the same time.

9 Hand-stitch the tassel loop up the mitered foldline at each corner, arranging the remaining part of the loop into a heart shape. Hand-stitch in place to finish. Press cloth on reverse before use.

SHORT BORDERED TABLECLOTH

*If you have a table with pretty legs that you would like to show off,
make this shorter circular variation.*

WHAT YOU WILL NEED

Fabric

Main piece
Diameter of table plus 20 in (50 cm) square

Border
8-in (20-cm) wide joined bias-cut strips (see p. 40) the
length of the circumference of the table plus 2 in (5 cm)

Accessories

Pencil

String

1 Cut the fabric as in Step 1, p.117, and pin joined bias-cut strips around outside edge of cloth, right sides together and raw edges aligned. Stitch, leaving a ⅝-in (1.5-cm) seam allowance.

2 When you are close to your starting point, remove work from machine and pin together the two ends of the bias strips where they meet. Stitch along the straight grain diagonally across the strips as shown.

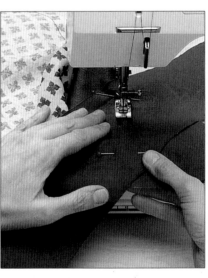

3 Trim the excess strip and continue stitching around outside edge of cloth, over the join. With the fabric wrong side up, press the border and the seam allowances away from the cloth (see inset).

4 Turn over a ⅝-in (1.5-cm) allowance on the border's outside edge, and press the border in half so the edge meets the stitch line. Slip-stitch (see p. 34) in place to finish. Press on reverse before use.

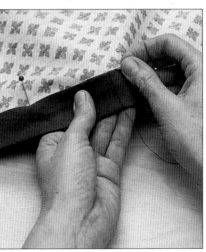

FITTED TABLE COVER

A FITTED TABLE COVER IS perfect for a plain table in a hallway or for a bedroom dressing table. Its defined shape creates a crisp, utilitarian feel, yet when coupled with a richly patterned fabric the overall effect is one of elegance and orderliness.

This clever idea for covering a table consists of full-length skirt panels cut to fit the sides of the table, plus decorative piping around the top of the cloth in a coordinating check. Although it looks as though there are inverted pleats at each corner, loose underlays are used so that the cover hangs free at the corners and is easily lifted to allow access to the contents underneath.

Pay attention to the easy-care properties of the fabric you choose, and select a fabric that coordinates with the other furnishings in your room. Here we used a closely woven printed cotton and made wide double hems around the skirt panels for extra weight, ensuring the skirt drapes correctly.

A cover like this can also disguise a rough shelf unit, an old cupboard, or even a chest or box. If you plan to use it to display flower vases or cosmetics, place a sheet of cut glass on top to protect the fabric.

WHAT YOU WILL NEED

Fabric

Top piece
Length of table plus $1\frac{1}{4}$ in (3 cm) x
width of table plus $1\frac{1}{4}$ in (3 cm)

Front and back skirts
Two pieces, each length of table plus 8 in (20 cm) x the
height of table plus $4\frac{5}{8}$ in (11.5 cm)

Side skirts
Two pieces, each width of table plus 8 in (20 cm) x the
height of the table plus $4\frac{5}{8}$ in (11.5 cm)

Underlays
Four pieces each 13 in (33 cm) x
the height of the table plus $4\frac{5}{8}$ in (11.5 cm)

Fabric for piping
2-in (5-cm) wide joined bias-cut strips (see p. 40) twice the
width of the table plus twice the length

Accessories

Piping cord
Twice the width of table plus twice the length, plus 6 in (15 cm)

Making the table cover

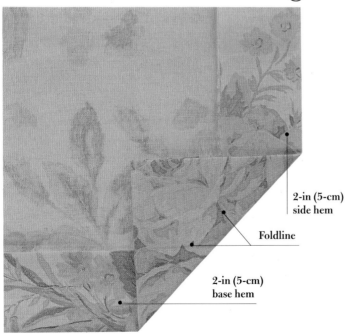

2-in (5-cm)
side hem

Foldline

2-in (5-cm)
base hem

1 On the bottom and side edge of each skirt panel, fold and press a 2-in (5-cm) double hem. To miter the bottom corners, open out the first fold of the hem and fold the corner in until the diagonal foldline crosses the pressed foldlines of the open hem.

2 Re-fold the hems to form a neat diagonal seam at each corner. Slipstitch around the three sides of each skirt, and along each mitered seam.

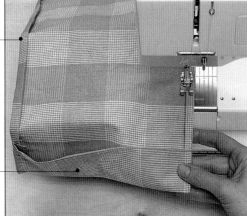

Hem turned over
¼ in (6 mm) and
then ⅜ in (1 cm)

2-in (5-cm)
double base hem

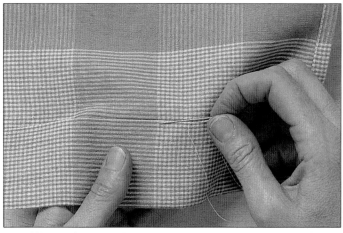

3 *On each underlay, press ¼-in (5-mm) and then ½-in (1-cm) hems down both sides. Fold a 2-in (5-cm) double hem along the bottom and press. Machine-stitch close to inside folded edge of side hems.*

4 *Slipstitch across the bottom hem, taking care that your stitches show as little as possible on the front of the fabric.*

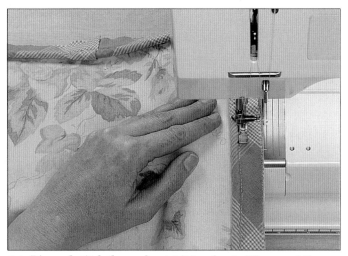

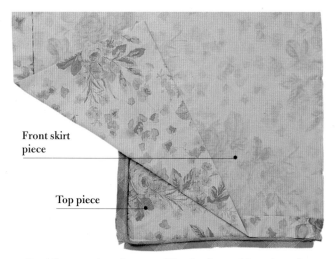

Front skirt
piece

Top piece

5 *Pin and stitch the made-up piping (see p.40) around the edges of the top piece on the right side. Start and finish the run at the back of the table, where it is less obtrusive.*

6 *Lay the top piece face up. Pin the front skirt piece, face down, to the top piece's front side, ensuring that it doesn't extend beyond the piping corners.*

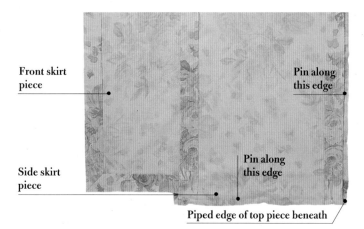

Front skirt
piece

Side skirt
piece

Pin along
this edge

Pin along
this edge

Piped edge of top piece beneath

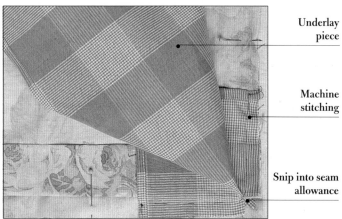

Underlay
piece

Machine
stitching

Snip into seam
allowance

7 *Pin a side skirt piece face down to the side of the top piece, again making sure that the edges don't extend beyond the piped corners.*

8 *Pin and baste an underlay piece face down over the corner, snipping into the seam allowance at the center point. Repeat steps 5, 6, and 7 until all the pieces of the skirt and underlays are in position. Using a zipper foot, machine-stitch close up against the piping to attach the skirt and underlays to the top. Press on reverse to finish.*

TIED FITTED TABLE COVER

Here is a simpler version of the fitted table cover that does without the loose underlays and has bow ties at each corner to secure the skirts.

WHAT YOU WILL NEED

Fabric

Top

As for main project (see p. 121)

Front and back skirts

Two pieces, each length of table plus 1¼ in (3 cm) x height of table plus 1¼ in (3 cm)

Side skirts

Two pieces, each width of table plus 1¼ in (3 cm) x height of table plus 1¼ in (3 cm)

Joined bias-cut strips

As for main project (see p. 121)

Ties

Eight strips each 14 in (35 cm) long (see p. 41)

Accessories

Piping cord

As for main project (see p. 121)

Top edge of skirt pieces

Machine stitching for 5 in (12.5 cm)

Seam allowance

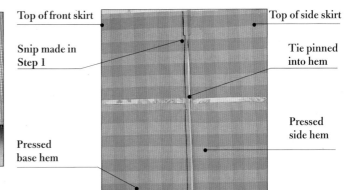

Top of front skirt

Top of side skirt

Snip made in Step 1

Tie pinned into hem

Pressed base hem

Pressed side hem

1 *Place a side skirt on top of front skirt (see Step 7 opposite), right sides together, aligning them along the top and down one side. Pin and stitch 5 in (12.5 cm) down the aligned side, ⅝ in (1.5 cm) in from edge. Snip into the allowance ⅝ in (1.5 cm) below the stitching end. Repeat to attach all skirts to each other in same way.*

2 *On each skirt, press over ¼ in (5 mm) then ½ in (1 cm) to back of fabric from snip down to bottom of skirt, along bottom and up to snip on other side. Tuck and pin a tie into the hem 10 in (25 cm) from snip on each side as shown.*

3 *Stitch close to inside fold of hem, around each skirt panel from snip to snip (see inset). Flip the ties out over the hems and stitch again around outside edges over the ties. Attach piping as in Step 5 opposite, and pin and stitch the skirt to top piece, right sides together.*

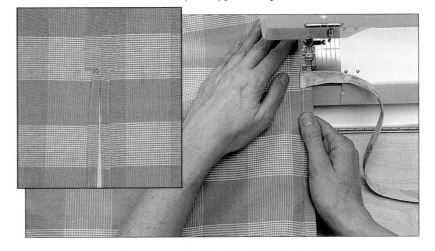

CARE AND REPAIR

Laundering

WHEN CHOOSING FABRICS for a project, it is very important to consider how it is to be cleaned. Determine if you will need to wash the finished piece regularly, such as a tablecloth, or dry-clean infrequently, such as a velvet cushion cover. Next, examine the care instructions for the fabric, if available – sometimes they are printed on the selvages of the fabric. Otherwise, ask the store staff about the qualities of the fabric, and exactly how it should be cleaned. If the fabric can be machine-washed, check if the colors will run and if it will shrink. If the fabric is not preshrunk, find out what the shrinkage percentage is and allow for this when estimating the amount you need. You must then prewash the fabric before sewing. However, bear in mind that some fabrics will always shrink a little when laundered. In the case of fitted covers, it is best to replace the pillow pad when the fabric is still slightly damp. This allows the fabric to stretch back into shape as it dries.

Lined items should always be dry-cleaned, as there is no guarantee that both fabrics will shrink equally when washed. This also applies to items that are trimmed with rope, fringe, and tassels.

Troubleshooting

WHEN YOU HAVE FINISHED a project, keep the leftover fabric. You can use fabric scraps to test out cleaning processes before you tackle the item itself, and to repair damages or stains. Leftovers will also help you color-match any new fabrics and furnishings you may want to add to your decor.

Although everyday wear and tear and soiling is inevitable, there are steps you can take to protect your work. Spray-on fabric protectors, used on cushions and upholstery, produce a water-repellant silicon finish, giving you time to wipe up spilled liquid before it soaks in and stains. Soft furnishings are often soiled by household dust, so use a low suction setting on your vacuum cleaner and clean regularly to prevent buildup.

For quick action on stains, there are commercial brands of upholstery cleaner and stain removers that work remarkably well on grease, wine, and coffee. If you prick your finger while sewing, there is a quick way to remove spots of blood: Simply moisten a length of cotton sewing thread with saliva and rub it against the spot.

INDEX

ACKNOWLEDGMENTS

Thanks to Cindy Richards for suggesting this book and Colin Ziegler for asking me to write it; to Emma Callery for her calming influence and Liz Dean and Sue Megginson for their attention to detail; to Geoff Dann for his patience; to Katarina Smith for finishing where I left off; and to Jeff Gilbert and Flynn Stacey for weathering many storms and giving me the time to do it.

Picture credits
pp. 12, 15: Elizabeth Whiting Associates